WHY YOU ~~SHOULD~~ <u>MUST</u> BECOME AN ENTREPRENEUR

WHY YOU ~~SHOULD~~ <u>MUST</u>
BECOME AN
ENTREPRENEUR

I will show you the way—
I have been there many times!

HAROLD L. MILLER

- ➢ TRUCK DRIVER
- ➢ RETAILER
- ➢ MANUFACTURER
- ➢ WHOLESALER
- ➢ SOLDIER
- ➢ LAWYER
- ➢ PROFESSOR
- ➢ BANKER
- ➢ REAL ESTATE DEVELOPER

ENTREPRENEURSHIP HALL OF FAME OF GREATER CHICAGO

iUniverse, Inc.
New York   Bloomington   Shanghai

WHY YOU ~~SHOULD~~ <u>MUST</u> BECOME AN ENTREPRENEUR
I will show you the way—I have been there many times!

iUniverse books may be ordered through booksellers or by contacting:

iUniverse, Inc.
1663 Liberty Drive
Bloomington, IN 47403
www.iuniverse.com
1-800-Authors (1-800-288-4677)

Because of the dynamic nature of the Internet, any Web addresses or links contained in this book may have changed since publication and may no longer be valid.

The views expressed in this work are solely those of the author and do not necessarily reflect the views of the publisher, and the publisher hereby disclaims any responsibility for them.

ISBN: 978-0-595-43742-9 (pbk)
ISBN: 978-0-595-88071-3 (ebk)

Printed in the United States of America

Why You Should Must Become an Entrepreneur is written from the vantage point of both an entrepreneur and lawyer—with over 50 years of experience in all facets of the business world.

In 1954, Harold Miller, with Joe Moss, established First Condominium Development Company (FCDC) and oversaw the first conversion of apartments to condominium units in the US. This original $900,000 project had eighteen units. FCDC in 1979 acquired Sandberg Village (Chicago), a 3.000-unit residential project, and completed conversion and sale in three 30-day marketing periods. In the process, real estate history was made. Acquisition price of the Sandberg Village was $105 million—reputedly the largest amount paid for a residential complex.

Entrepreneurs must learn to ...

- Negotiate with banks
- Formulate business plans
- Establish a credit file
- Structure the business (partnership? incorporate?)
- Hire lawyers, accountants, financial advisors
- Decide when to merge or be acquired, retire and move on
- Maintain executive control or determine a worthy successor

Why You Should Must Become an Entrepreneur guides you through these practical tasks and more—siting examples from the most famous entrepreneurships of our time: Starbucks, Microsoft, Domino's Pizza, Google, Kinko's, Xerox and eBay among others.

CONTENTS

ACKNOWLEDGEMENTS   xiii

INTRODUCTION   xv

ABOARD THE GOOD SHIP H.M. ENTREPRENEURSHIP   xvi

STARTING YOUR OWN JOURNEY   xvii

WHAT IS AN ENTREPRENEUR?   xvii

DO YOU HAVE WHAT IT TAKES?   xviii

THE ENTREPRENEURIAL FORMULA   xviii

SECTION I   1

CASE STUDIES FOR THE STUDENT ENTREPRENEUR   1

PEOPLE LOOK BUT THEY DON'T SEE OPPORTUNITIES   2

TABLE ONE   3

MY PERSONAL JOURNEY AS AN ENTREPRENEUR   4

    MILLER FURNITURE COMPANY, ESTABLISHED 1940   4

    RETURNING FROM WORLD WAR II—
    AND RESUMING MY CAREER   6

    FIRST CONDOMINIUM DEVELOPMENT COMPANY   7

CASE STUDIES   10

    STARBUCKS   10

    DOMINO'S PIZZA   13

    ELECTRIC TOOTHBRUSH   15

    PASTE-ON FINGERNAILS   18

VELCRO   20

KINKO'S   22

XEROX CORPORATION   24

MICROSOFT   25

HEWLETT PACKARD   27

GOOGLE   29

eBAY   31

AMERICAN RARITIES COINS   33

PETERSEN REALTY COMPANY, CHICAGO   35

ENTREPRENEURSHIP WITHIN YOUR EMPLOYMENT   37

TWO ENTREPRENEURSHIPS THAT FAILED   38

MOTOROLA—IRIDIUM   38

BACH PIANO COMPANY   40

REVIEW, DISCUSSION AND QUESTIONS   42

LESSONS LEARNED FROM THE TWO FAILURES   42

ASSESSING DEMAND (examples)   42

HIGHLY SPECIALIZED TRAINING AND BRAIN POWER   43

THE NEED TO BE YOUR OWN BOSS   43

INVENTORS   43

TWO THAT FAILED MANUFACTURING   43

NECESSITIES FOR ALL ENTREPRENEURS   43

SECTION II   **51**

WELCOME TO THE WIDE, PROFITABLE AND (POTENTIALLY)
HAZARDOUS WORLD OF BUSINESS   51

YOUR BUSINESS AND YOUR BUSINESS PLAN   51

WHAT TYPE OF BUSINESS 52

OBJECTIVE OF THE BUSINESS PLAN 52

WHO ARE THE PRINCIPALS 52

NOW PAY ATTENTION CLASS! 53

NECESSARY ENTREPRENEURIAL INGREDIENTS 55

A. ACCOUNTING FIRM 55

B. MARKET RESEARCH 56

C. ADVERTISING 57

D. PUBLIC RELATIONS 58

BRINGING YOUR STORY TO THE PUBLIC 58

CRISIS MANAGEMENT 58

ASK YOUR BANKER FOR RECOMMENDATIONS 60

E. ATTORNEYS 60

BBB—BANKS, BANKERS AND BROKERS 61

DO NOT PUT ALL OF YOUR EGGS INTO
ONE (BANK) BASKET 62

BUSINESS HAZARDS: A PERSONAL EXPERIENCE 66

WILLOUGBY, CHEVY CHASE, MARYLAND 66

YOUR CREDIT FILE 68

BROKERS 69

VENTURE CAPITALISTS 70

STOCKBROKERS 71

FINANCIAL ADVISORS 71

REAL ESTATE BROKERS 71

STRUCTURING YOUR BUSINESS 72

PARTNERSHIPS 72

LIMITED PARTNERSHIPS 72

PROPRIETORSHIP 73

CORPORATIONS 73

THE MANY HAZARDS 73

EXECUTIVES: IMPROVING YOUR PERFORMANCE 75

PROBLEM SOLVING: A DIFFICULT AND COMMON
OCCURRENCE 75

ABRAHAM LINCOLN METHOD 76

ANDREW CARNEGIE 76

PERSONAL MEMORANDUMS 77

RETURNING PHONE CALLS 77

HOLIDAY CARDS 78

BOARD OF DIRECTORS: SHOULD I JOIN
OR SHOULD I NOT 78

HOW WE LOST THE WAR TO JAPAN (AUTOS) 78

LESSONS FROM THREE GIANTS OF INDUSTRY 79

ABRAHAM N. PRITZKER 79

CHARLES ALLEN 81

ARTHUR RUBLOFF 83

CONGRATULATIONS! NOW, WHAT ABOUT YOUR FUTURE? 85

1. CASH IN YOUR CHIPS? 85

2. RETIREMENT—WHAT A WONDERFUL OPPORTUNITY 85

3. BE ACQUIRED 86

4. SHOULD I STAY WITH THE NEW COMPANY? 86

5. SHOULD I ACQUIRE ANOTHER COMPANY? 87

6. GOING PUBLIC 87

A NEW DIRECTION FOR AMERICAN ENTREPRENEURSHIP   87

APPENDIX   89

PROMISSORY NOTE PROVISIONS REQUIRED BY THE LENDER   89

FACTS FOR ESTABLISHING A REAL ESTATE OFFICE   91

SAMPLE BUSINESS PLAN   95

MANDATORY READING   108

SUGGESTED READING   108

RESOURCES FOR THE RESOURCEFUL ENTREPRENEUR   110

    BOOKS   110

    PUBLICATIONS   110

    OTHER WEB SOURCES   111

ACKNOWLEDGEMENTS

This book is the result of approximately 65 years as an attorney at law, professor and entrepreneur. I cannot remember or acknowledge all of the people who have played major roles in my achievements during this long period of time. Forgive me if you are not mentioned.

First and foremost, this book is dedicated to my wife of over 57 years, Beatrice Kraus Miller. She has encouraged and directed me during my many business ventures.

This book is also a tribute to the memory of Dean Noble Lee who enabled returning World War II veterans like myself to receive one year of college credit for each year of military service and to attorney Joe Moss who became my partner when we formed First Condominium Development Company (FCDC). In 1965 we became the first realtors in the U.S. to convert an apartment building into condominiums.

My thanks to former colleagues and professors at the University of Illinois, Chicago: John McDonald, Director, Center of Urban Real Estate and former Dean of the School of Business; Gerald Hills, Director, Institute for Entrepreneurial Studies; and Dean S.G. (Woody) Huneryager, former head of the university's Management Department, College of Business, who appointed me adjunct professor in the School of Business where I served for ten years.

And a thanks to the many others who provided encouragement and advice, including Bernard Baum, Leo Shapiro, Al Rafelson, Tad Simons, Dr. Lenore Novar, and Connie Heneghan.

Last but not least, this is a memorial to Abraham N. Pritzker (widely known as simply "A.N.") and his brother Jack, founders of the Pritzker empire, and Arthur Rubloff, whose contributions to commercial real estate changed the face of Chicago.

Harold L. Miller
Evanston, IL
hlrellim@sbcglobal.net
www.entrepreneurship-why.com

INTRODUCTION

During the winter of 2004-2005, at a pancake house in Highland Park, IL, a man in his mid-thirties wearing a business suit seated me. I was shocked and he saw that I was shocked.

"What did you do before you had this job?" I asked.

"I was in middle management," he replied.

I thought to myself, "Here is a man who is educated, has a degree of success and now his job is gone, possibly forever. Why doesn't he take matters into his own hands and become an entrepreneur?"

Then it occurred to me that even if he wanted to become an entrepreneur, he might not know how. I have been an entrepreneur since age nineteen and taught entrepreneurship at the University of Illinois (Chicago) School of Business for approximately ten years as an adjunct professor. "Why don't I write a book that could help this fellow?" I thought.

This book is the culmination of that effort and a result of my sixty-five years of experience as an entrepreneur. I feel that it can assist the many thousands who are looking to the future with a great deal of anxiety and worry. The world that I knew is gone, except for memories. The path of my children, all in their fifties, is already clear. But for the younger generation the working world can be a strange and intimidating place. Gone are the days when one would be employed by just one company and receive a pension upon retirement. Career paths are much more fragmented now, yet there are also many more options, including the very satisfying option of becoming an entrepreneur.

As you will see, entrepreneurship can take many forms. The idea for a company or innovation can come from anywhere, and success or failure will ultimately depend on many factors. But all successful entrepreneurs share certain common traits of character, such as passion and perseverance, and all depend upon a certain amount of luck, or serendipity, to go along with their hard work. My hope is that anyone who reads the following pages will find in them a moment or two of serendipity as well—or at least a spark of enthusiasm for embracing both the challenges and rewards of entrepreneurship.

Section I is by far most important, for it explores the path to success of seventeen different entrepreneurs. Their stories serve as a basis for discussion, and from their examples you will learn how to begin this challenging journey.

Section II deals with the development of your entrepreneurial business. This is practical information that you will need in order to develop a business plan, acquire start-up capital and manage the growth of your budding enterprise. A guide to additional resources is also included.

ABOARD THE GOOD SHIP H.M. ENTREPRENEURSHIP

I was a professor of entrepreneurship at the University of Illinois, Chicago for ten years, so in Section I will be using the format used in my classroom. The first thing I always said to my students was: "Congratulations! You are now enrolled in my master class on how to become an entrepreneur. Join me aboard the Good Ship H.M. Entrepreneurship and we will begin our journey ... Join me for a voyage of discovery."

I have been an entrepreneur all my life. The Good Ship Entrepreneurship has taken me many places and provided me with many important life lessons. My voyage as Captain started at age nineteen and continued for over sixty years.

Every entrepreneur is the captain of his own ship. But every Captain must have a First Mate. My most capable First Mate has been my wife of over fifty-six years. Together, we have voyaged through life, through the storms and long periods of happiness, success and blessings. Following are the major ports we encountered on our voyage:

Port #1 Opened the Miller Furniture Company in Chicago at the age of nineteen.

Port #2 World War II: Enlisted shortly after Pearl Harbor was attacked. I wanted to repay this country for the many blessings it had given to my parents who had come here from a viciously anti-Semitic and backward Russia. I served approximately three years in the European Theatre of Operations in the Ground Crew of a fighter group in England, France and Germany. I saw it all and lived to tell about it.

Port #3 Established wholesale business of shipping upright pianos and useful appliances to retail stores in Southern states. This opportunity arose after the war. Factories in the North that had produced war goods began producing consumer goods. The large northern population had the opportunity to replace useful but outdated pianos and appliances needed by consumers in the Southern states. So I started supplying retail stores from Tennessee westward to Texas with these products and liquidated the business when northern factories began delivering directly to the South.

Port #4 Established a series of retail piano stores.

Port #5 Married my first mate and attended law school.

Port #6   Became a successful lawyer, specializing in real estate.

Port #7   Began converting apartment buildings into condominiums, which became an extremely lucrative business.

Port #8   Addressed sub-committee of the U.S. Congress to explain the advantages, both to renters and to the community, of converting apartment buildings into condominiums.

Port #9   In 1993, I was appointed Professor (Adjunct) in the School of Business, University of Illinois, Chicago. I taught a course in entrepreneurship, real estate finance, and negotiations. It was one of the most rewarding periods of my life.

Port #10 The Great Ship H.M. Entrepreneurship docked after its final voyage in approximately 1983, upon the birth of our first grandchild. My wife and I, both from humble circumstances, had worked a long, hard and successful life together. It was time to end our voyage of entrepreneurship.

STARTING YOUR OWN JOURNEY

One of the reasons I wrote this book is that the path of entrepreneurship, though not for everyone, has provided me with an extremely fulfilling life, and I wanted to share that sense of fulfillment and possibility with as many people as possible. Before you get started as an entrepreneur, however, you must decide if it's really what you want to do. Understand, this is not a nine-to-five job. It will require many hours of hard work, and there will be periods of frustration, but you can be successful, and you can be your own boss.

Below is a list of questions that you should answer as truthfully as possible. If your answers to these questions are negative, this book may not help you. If your answers are positive, keep reading—this book was written for you.

WHAT IS AN ENTREPRENEUR?

An entrepreneur is a person who perceives a demand for a product/service and proceeds to develop the product/service that will meet that demand. The process involves developing a quality product, raising the initial start-up capital and developing the business to support the production and sale of the product/service.

DO YOU HAVE WHAT IT TAKES?

Becoming an entrepreneur is not easy, but the rewards can be great. Here are a few personal questions you must ask of yourself:

1. Am I primarily a detail person or am I a person with vision? (An entrepreneur must be both: a visionary who can keep track of details.)

2. Do I have the resources to forego a Friday paycheck until my business becomes profitable?

3. Will my spouse go along with the ups, downs, and uncertainties of entrepreneurial life?

4. Am I the type of person who continues to fight until success is achieved, no matter how many times I get knocked down?

5. Do I accept advice freely and adjust the advice to my own experience and needs?

6. Am I comfortable taking risks that could potentially fail?

7. Do I have the capital resources for initial start-up?

If your truthful responses to the above questions were positive, you may indeed have the character and fortitude it takes to be successful. Once you have an idea upon which you can base a business, you will utilize the following basic formula—which we'll cover extensively as we go along—to realize your entrepreneurial dream.

THE ENTREPRENEURIAL FORMULA

1. Discover a subject (product or service) for which there is a demand.

2. Provide or acquire the initial start-up capital.

3. Find a reliable partner.

4. Never give up—keep going.

5. Obtain outside financing through sources such as venture capitalists or banks.

6. Hire an experienced accountant early on. (At this stage, an accountant is more important than a lawyer.)

7. Hire an experienced lawyer to draw up business documents.

8. Form a small corporation. This will give you both flexibility and control as the corporation grows.

My own voyage included becoming a lawyer. Learning to be a lawyer involves the study of cases, understanding the facts and elements of a controversy, as well as the over-arching principles and final conclusions of any given case.

We'll study the case histories of seventeen entrepreneurs, and by doing so, will discover:

A. How to identify and fulfill demand for a product.

B. What Inspiration and Vision look and feel like.

C. How to build and sustain confidence.

D. Where to acquire initial start-up capital.

E. The importance of developing a quality product.

F. Why a good partner can make all the difference.

G. How motivation and passion lead to success.

H. The role of persistence and faith in overcoming obstacles.

SECTION I

CASE STUDIES FOR THE STUDENT ENTREPRENEUR

In this section, you, the Student Entrepreneur, will be presented with seventeen case studies. Fifteen of these are examples of entrepreneurial success, and the last two examples of business failures. Every case is presented to you as if you were an actual student in my classroom. We'll briefly review case histories in order to understand why the entrepreneurs ventured into their businesses, and we'll also explore the role of **serendipity** behind each entrepreneur's circumstances. The review will be followed by a detailed list of the Key Facts and Key Lessons you should take with you from each case study.

> **Serendipity**: *the act of making a beneficial discovery, and having the sagacity, or wisdom, to recognize the discovery as fortunate and beneficial*

You'll notice that many of the case studies include major U.S. companies, while others are about *ideas* that entrepreneurs pursued and (in some instances) sold to larger companies to the benefit of the individual entrepreneur.

Here is the list of the companies we will be studying:

Miller Furniture Company
First Condominium Development Company
Starbucks
Domino's Pizza
Electric Toothbrush
Paste-On Fingernails
Velcro
Kinko's

Xerox Corporation
Microsoft
Hewlett Packard
Google
eBay
American Rarities Coins
Petersen Realty Co., Chicago
Motorola—Iridium
Bach Piano Company

Miller Furniture Co., American Rarities Coins, Peterson Realty, Starbucks, Domino's Pizza, Paste-On Fingernails, Kinko's, First Condominium Development Co., and Bach Piano Co. are examples of companies started by entrepreneurs because they wished to become self-employed. They all wanted to be "the head and not the tail" of their new enterprise. These people discovered a demand for their product, and they were able to meet the initial capital requirements on their own, or with the help of family and friends.

Microsoft, eBay, Electric toothbrush, Xerox, Hewlett Packard, Google, Motorola-Iridium are examples of entrepreneurs who founded companies because they were highly skilled in special areas of knowledge. With these tools, they were able to discover a product for which there would be a demand. Except for Xerox and Motorola-Iridium, the initial capital requirements were primarily the imagination, vision and hard work to develop their respective products.

PEOPLE LOOK BUT THEY DON'T SEE OPPORTUNITIES

In this section, you will be looking *into the eyes and minds* of seventeen entrepreneurs to learn how they saw their world and identified the opportunity around which they built their businesses. Also, we'll see how the opportunity was discovered, developed, and fulfilled. Again, we'll make special note of how individuals used serendipity to their advantage. These entrepreneurs saw opportunity where others did not. Identifying opportunity when it knocks and knowing when to answer is a key component of entrepreneurship!

By thoroughly studying Section One, you will come to understand that opportunities exist everywhere. What you choose to do with these opportunities is the key factor that will determine whether your entrepreneurial venture is successful. Many people can think of things that the world needs, but few of them have the fortitude and ambition to do what's necessary to fill that need. They would prefer that someone else do it, which is okay—because that someone might be you!

TABLE ONE

Table One briefly recaps the highlights of each case study, showing whether the entrepreneur made a modification to an existing product, invented a product, whether he or she was supplying a demand for said product, whether the venture was a success, and how much capital was originally required.

THROUGH THE EYES AND INTO THE MINDS OF SEVENTEEN ENTREPRENEURS

BRIEF SUMMARY

SUBJECT	MODIFICATION	INVENTION	DEMAND	SUCCESS	CAPITAL REQUIRED
1. Starbucks	X		X	X	LESS THAN $5,000
2. Domino's Pizza	X		X	X	LESS THAN $5,000
3. Electric Toothbrush		X	X	X	Less than one million
4. Paste-on Fingernails		X	X	X	$5,000
5. Velcro		X	X	X	Less than $2,000
6. Kinko's Proprietorship	X		X	X	Less than $5,000
7. Xerox		X	X	X	Less than one million
8. Microsoft	X		X	X	Less than $10,000
9. Hewlett Packard	X		X	X	Less than $1,000
10. Google	X		X	X	Less than $5,000
11. eBay	X		X	X	Less than $5,000
12. Condo Conversions	X		X	X	$100,000
13. Motorola Iridium	X		X	Failure	Approximately $5 Billion
14. Bach Piano Co.	X		X	Failure	$100,000
15. American Rarity Coins	X		X	X	Less than $25,000
16. Miller Furniture Co.	X		X	X	$25,000
17. Peterson Realty Co.	X		X	X	Less than $25,000

REVIEW

The case studies in this section will be followed by a detailed summary and the sort of discussion questions that my students would typically ask. The give and take of the classroom is missing, unfortunately, but the information is still quite valuable.

MY PERSONAL JOURNEY AS AN ENTREPRENEUR

MILLER FURNITURE COMPANY, ESTABLISHED 1940

Let's begin with my own story, which gives you, the student, an opportunity to become better acquainted with me. I have been an entrepreneur all my life. Even though there have been numerous challenges and setbacks along the way, the rewards have far outweighed the negatives. My hope is that by telling you my story you will have a keener understanding of how I learned the lessons of entrepreneurship, and why they must be passed along to you.

At age sixteen, during the summer months, I became a delivery truck driver. It provided me with spending money and it was hard work. But I knew that this was not to be my future. I completed one year at a community college with a major in accounting. My instructor wisely suggested that I did not have the necessary facility for this profession. My parents were unable to give me any direction, inasmuch they were Russian immigrants.

My father had a small moving business and engaged, on a limited scale, in the buying and selling of used furniture. I recognized that my own future lay in the retail furniture business, for which there is always a demand. In 1940, at age nineteen, I opened a small retail furniture store on Madison Street, one of Chicago's major thoroughfares and well known. With borrowed capital from my parents, I learned the essential ingredients of a retail business. It was a success. I was able to meet all of my obligations and drew a moderate salary. I did the buying, selling, advertising, bookkeeping, window displays, assisted with delivery, cleaning, dusting and all of the other functions of a retail operation. A big operation has the same elements, but on a larger scale. This small retail operation gave me invaluable knowledge of how to run a business in all its details and enabled me, in later years, to become a successful and wealthy businessman.

We were competing with a larger retail furniture store nearby. I frequently received new customers who came to my store because the owner had said, "Don't go to Miller Furniture Company." Here's a key piece of advice: never knock your competitor. Always have something nice to say, or say nothing.

At some point during the year 1941, I met Mr. Rhinnsberger, a businessman who had become a small financier. He recognized that most small manufacturers are undercapitalized and frequently had difficulty meeting their Friday payrolls, and could find themselves out of business by Monday. On Thursdays, he would visit these small manufacturers, usually in the upholstered furniture and bedding industry, and buy up the inventory that was ready for shipment.

Frequently, the manufacturer would sell his inventory at a sharply discounted price so he could meet his Friday payroll. Mr. Rhinnsberger always paid immediately. He consigned the discounted inventory to me, thus providing my retail operation with a steady supply of upholstered furniture, bedding, sofa beds and similar items. Because of my limited capital, I was able to purchase inventory, remain in business and sell these products far below the usual retail price.

My relationship with Mr. Rhinnsberger is a great example of *serendipity*. Not only did our arrangement fill the gap in the capital requirements for my retail operation and solve his payroll problems, it came at precisely the right time for both of us. Seeing the opportunity, we seized it. Mr. Rhinnsberger was a few years younger than my own father, and thereafter undertook to become a personal mentor of mine.

With the outbreak of World War II, December 7, 1941, I liquidated my furniture business and volunteered to serve my country. For a period of approximately three years, I was a member of the 9th Air Force Fighter Group Ground Crew in England, France and Germany.

In keeping with our presentation format, I have given you the brief summary and now we'll follow up with a review of the Key Facts and the Key Lessons.

KEY FACTS

1. After deciding that a career in truck driving was not in my future, opened a retail furniture store.

2. My father provided the initial capital of $10,000.

3. Locating near a large competitor can attract customers to your business.

4. A thorough course in accounting is essential for your future in the business world.

5. Lessons learned from the proprietorship of a small business will enable you to enter the business world on a larger scale at a later date.

6. Capital needs for inventory can be provided by a financier, banks or investors.

7. Retailing enabled me to become a successful business lawyer. Most lawyers have no training in business. I recognized that many of my clients' problems were either business or legal problems with major business overtones.

8. With the outbreak of the Second World War, I liquidated my business, volunteered for the Air Force and served for approximately three years.

KEY LESSONS

1. Demanded more out of life than being a truck driver.

2. Determined to be my own boss.

3. Repaid this country for the freedoms given to my immigrant parents.

4. Choose a product for which there is always a demand (furniture, in my case).

5. Start-up capital can come from family and friends.

6. Looking around at family history: father's moving business involved the buying and selling of used furniture.

7. Located the business on a major thoroughfare easily recognizable by the public.

8. Successful, albeit difficult, learning business operations.

9. Never, ever give up.

10. A partner can bring capital, ideas and support.

11. Fortuitous source of capital, Mr. Rhinnsberger.

12. Undercapitalized manufacturers are forced to sell their product at a substantial discount in order to meet their payrolls.

13. This enabled Miller Furniture to sell recognized products at prices far below the competitors.

14. In business, money represents power. (Mr. Rhinnsberger)

15. Important lessons can be learned from difficult experiences encountered in the business world.

RETURNING FROM WORLD WAR II—AND RESUMING MY CAREER

After returning from the service, I continued on as an entrepreneur, utilizing lessons I had learned running my previous business. I also made use of my experiences and observations while in the service.

I received my military training in the South, where many similar bases were located. Because of this, the area received a vast influx of capital and wartime factories during this period. Historically, however, the South had generally had an agricultural economic foundation with only a small industrial base.

When the war ended in 1945, the production of consumer goods was resumed. Most factories, along with a greater percentage of the U.S. population, were located in the North. Factories undertook to fulfill the demand for consumer goods, supplying the northern population first. Only after consumer demand in the North was met were goods then sold to southern merchants. Demand was high, since production of consumer goods had been at a virtual standstill from the beginning of the Great Depression in 1929 until the end of World War II, in 1945.

Observations during my military training in the South enabled me to recognize that while people in the North wanted to replace out-dated items with new, contemporary goods, folks in the South demanded the old products. For three years after the war, I established a network of dealers in the southern states who purchased the older items and used my delivery trucks to send the goods down South.

In addition to such things as plumbing equipment and cooking ranges, upright pianos were being replaced in the North by spinet pianos, which were smaller and more attractive to consumers at the time. In 1948, I established a retail piano store in Chicago's South Side and the following year opened one in Chicago's Near North Side. During that same year, I enrolled in John Marshall Law School's evening classes. I married my wife, Beatrice Kraus Miller, in 1950—the beginning of a 57-year relationship.

In 1950, I ended all my business activities, with the exception of the retail piano store, and completed my law school studies. By 1955, a successful law practice had been established, specializing in real estate. Shortly afterward, I became a member of the Chicago Bar Association Real Estate Section.

FIRST CONDOMINIUM DEVELOPMENT COMPANY

1964 saw the passage of the Illinois Condominium Property Act, and I became a member of the first sub-committee on condominiums of the Chicago Bar Association. That same year, attorney Joe Moss and I converted the *first* apartment building into condominiums in the continental U.S. Thus began the First Condominium Development Company (FCDC), established in 1965.

Joe was an important partner. Joe had come by my office to discuss a pending legal matter. He happened to see a declaration of condominium on my desk, which I was preparing. Joe asked me if I'd given any thought to converting an existing building into condominiums. The **BRIGHT LIGHT** of *serendipity* flashed on: I recognized that the conversion of existing apartment buildings into condominiums would succeed on a national scale. Purchasing condominiums was a great way for people to gain ownership in real estate and enjoy the many benefits that accrue with ownership. I had expertise in condominiums, finances and mortgages; Joe took on the rehabilitation and sales of the apartments. In 1965, at the corner of 55th and Everett Streets, in Hyde Park, we acquired an eighteen-unit apartment building for about $360,000 on an option, with the right to convert to condos. Payment to the owner for the conversion option was approximately $10,000, and conversion costs came in at about $25,000. The capital was provided by the two partners, Joe Moss and me. **This was the first time an apartment building was converted into condominiums in the United States.**

This first conversion was a long and difficult process. Condominiums were such a new concept that not even the financial institutions had heard of them. Insights into profit potential resulted in being able to convince the owner of the apartment building to grant us the conversion option for less than $5,000. The primary costs involved upgrading the nearly sixty-year-old apartment building. Ultimately the conversion was a success. I told Joe that if we could convert two or three more buildings we could convince the financial markets that condominium conversions were a new and important introduction into residential real estate. There was little doubt that every metropolitan area in the U.S. had older rental buildings that could eventually be converted to condominiums. We did make money, but the main profit was in the learning experience, which led FCDC into the future. We learned that the potential benefits of the venture far outweighed the risks.

Because of my experience with my clients Jack Stone and Fred Allen, who had constructed the first condominium in Illinois, in Oak Park, in 1966-67, I gained valuable legal and business knowledge in the new condominium business that I could apply to FCDC.

FCDC went on to develop and convert other apartment complexes. The Narragansett, in Chicago, was the first high-rise ever converted into condominiums, around 1968. 1969 saw the first conversion of an apartment building in Evanston, Illinois. In 1972, FCDC went on to convert buildings in Miami, New York City, and other cities in the U.S. Mr. Moss resigned from FCDC in approximately 1979 and continued conversions in Philadelphia, Chicago and other cities as well.

In 1979, I purchased Sandburg Village, in Chicago, for $105 million, which at that time was the highest price ever paid for a residential project in the U.S. Arthur Rubloff was the spokesman for a twenty-one-member partnership and had the authority to select the buyer. I had purchased a major apartment building from Mr. Rubloff several years earlier, in Hyde Park, on an installment contract basis. The eventual price paid to Mr. Rubloff and his partners, the Allen brothers, was higher than his original asking price, which made Mr. Rubloff quite happy.

I performed the necessary evaluation of the value of the approximately 3,000 units and recognized that the acquisition price represented a fair value. A careful study revealed that the conversion could be very successful and profitable. Continental Illinois National Bank, one of the nation's largest banks, provided the funding.

Abraham Pritzker (A.N.), co-founder of the Pritzker family empire, contacted me about becoming a partner in the venture. I realized that it would be of great importance to have A.N. as a partner, because of his stature in the financial world. It was a fifty-fifty partnership. A.N. had confidence in me, and was kept fully informed on a daily basis regarding the progress of the conversion. I have always practiced full disclosure with my various partners on a steady, ongoing basis.

In order to upgrade the buildings and meet advertising and sales expenses, we required an additional $15 million. First Federal Savings of Chicago, at that time the largest savings and loan association in Illinois, approached me and offered to become a partner in the project and invest additional funds in exchange for 25% of the profits. After consulting with A.N., we agreed to accept First Federal's partnership offer.

The conversion of Sandburg Village was a phenomenal success, with the partners receiving a return of their capital after the closing of Phase One, consisting of four buildings. We converted 2,600 units into condominiums in three 30-day marketing periods.

FCDC continued to develop and convert other properties. In 1982, we converted 760 units in Willoughby, Chevy Chase, Maryland, an upscale suburb of Washington, D.C. Another project was the conversion of The Century, in Midtown Manhattan. Conversions of existing apartment buildings, hotels and office buildings are now a common practice throughout the United States. People prefer to own instead of being lifetime renters. The famous Wrigley office building on Chicago's Magnificent Mile as well as the Plaza Hotel in Manhattan are being converted to condominiums.

Without my original partner, Joe Moss, I probably never would have become an entrepreneur in condo conversions. All the partners I worked with brought into the partnerships capital, support, questioning, confidence, hard work and the drive to succeed.

CASE STUDIES

STARBUCKS

Coffee is a beverage in great demand. It is the national drink. (More than half of all Americans drink it, and the average coffee drinker enjoys three to four cups a day.)

With less than $5,000 starting capital, partners Gordon Bowker, Jerry Baldwin and Zev Siegl opened a Starbucks coffee shop in Seattle, WA in 1971. By 1982, they had expanded to five coffee shops. Theirs was strictly a local operation. The partners recognized that a consumer would pay a high price for an outstanding cup of delicious coffee, a fact confirmed by the expansion of the coffee shops from one to five. The partners established and maintained the highest standards for quality coffee. Coffee beans more than eight days old were either discarded or donated to charity.

A wholesale division called Carvali was established. Howard Schultz was appointed manager of retail operations in 1982. In 1983, while vacationing in Italy, Schultz discovered the Italian-style coffee shops, which he was convinced would be successful in the hectic society of the United States. The Italian coffee bars offered a quiet place to relax, converse and sip a good cup of coffee.

The owners of Starbucks were not convinced. Schultz resigned and opened under the name of Il Giornale, featuring the Italian-style coffee shop. Because it was extremely successful, the owners of Starbucks finally bought into the concept. A new Starbucks location with the Italian-style coffee bar followed and received overwhelming consumer acceptance.

In order to maintain the quality and integrity of the coffee, a roasting plant was established in 1972. The wholesale division was sold in 1987 to concentrate on Starbucks coffee shops. Schultz's company, Il Giornale, purchased Starbucks for $4 million and he became chairman, CEO and president. The original Starbucks coffee shop would have remained a local operation had it not recognized the tremendous demand for an Italian-style coffee shop that could exist in the US (*serendipity*). By 2001, guided by Schultz's brilliant management, Starbucks grew tremendously and consisted of more than 100,000 employees.

It may interest your to know, there were approximately 2,200 Starbucks locations in North America by the year 2000. Foreign locations were also established in Europe and Japan. Future expansion was being planned for China. In countries where tea was popular, quality tea was also added to the menu. The quality of all Starbucks products was always maintained and roasting plants were opened throughout the world.

Starbucks is essentially a fast-food operation. The employees are well-trained and, because of benefits such as the opportunity to buy stock and health insurance, the employees are satisfied, and this satisfaction shows in how they treat their customers.

The sale of coffee by the cup is extremely profitable. In the Chicago area, a cup of Starbucks sells for approximately $1.60. The ingredients, including the paper cup, cream, stirrer, napkins and so on cost approximately seven cents. With the addition of cream and ice, mixed in a blender and a sophisticated name, the selling price increases to about $3.50. The total cost is approximately fifteen cents. Espresso coffee was also introduced, which sells for approximately $3.50, with a total production cost of approximately fifteen cents per serving. These amazingly high profit margins enabled Starbucks to expand. Their major operating cost is rent, but because of the extreme profit and high sales volume, the overall profitability of the company is maintained. Coffee beans are also sold in bulk for approximately $10 per pound, with an actual cost of about $1 per pound.

The first successful public offering was by NASDAQ in 1992. Starbucks continues to grow through other outlets, such as distribution through food chains and coffee bars in various retail establishments such as Nordstrom, Barnes and Noble and other venues. Coffee bags are now available in supermarkets throughout the country.

Licensing agreements are made through franchising. Additional Starbucks-owned outlets continue to grow. In addition to coffee by the cup and in bulk, revenues are also generated by the sale of sweets, mugs and espresso machines. Pepsi Cola began distributing Starbucks coffee drinks in bottles, another highly profitable product. "Have you had your Starbucks today?" is a very effective slogan now widely accepted.

Because of its superior product and great demand, Starbuck's revenue and profits increased tremendously, from a 1993 profit of approximately $48 million on revenues of approximately $176 million, to a profit of approximately $58 million on revenues of $960 million by 1997. They took a common beverage and made it into a national name brand.

The original three partners, with small capital, were seeking to enter into the business world. They recognized the demand for coffee and never envisioned that the company would grow to become a major U.S. corporation. This was due to Howard Schultz, who purchased the company and had the foresight, determination, vision and managerial skills. In 2000, net income was approximately $102 million on sales of $1.7 billion.

KEY FACTS

1. The four partners combined their capital of less than $5,000 to enter the business world.

2. They were confident that their local coffee shops would be successful by delivering an outstanding cup of coffee for which the consumer would pay a high price.

3. Howard Schultz, a partner, after visiting the coffee shops in Milan, Italy, recognized that there would be a great demand in the U.S. for a leisure coffee bar, outstanding coffee and excellent service. (*serendipity*)

4. Schultz, already the owner of Il Giornale coffee shops, combined the two under "Starbucks" and became the sole owner. With his great managerial skills, he expanded Starbucks to become a national company.

5. The highest standards for quality coffee had already been established and roasting plants were created throughout the world in order to provide fresh coffee beans to the outlets. Beans older than eight days were either donated to charity or discarded.

6. Growth continued because of the extremely high profits and tremendous demand. The first outside capital was through a NASDAQ public offering in 1992.

7. Starbucks became a major U.S. corporation with sales in 2000 of $1.7 billion and a profit of $102 million.

8. Recognizing there would be worldwide demand, franchising was established in Europe. In Asian countries, outstanding tea was also offered.

KEY LESSONS

1. Low start-up capital can be sufficient.

2. Partners can complement and support one another with capital, motivation, determination and ideas.

3. Recognizing what other cultures had to offer that could be in great demand in the U.S. led Starbucks to establish a Milan-style coffee bar in the U.S.

4. It was a fast food operation with highly trained and happy service employees who can invest in the company.

5. The integrity of the product was established and maintained throughout its history internationally.

6. The public will pay a high price for an outstanding product.

7. A successful business will depend upon outstanding management skills of the chief executive.

DOMINO'S PIZZA

In 1960, brothers Tom and Jim Monaghan purchased a bankrupt pizza parlor named DomiNick's in Ypsilanti, Michigan for $500. They recognized that pizza is a tasty and highly nutritious food, widely accepted throughout the U.S. Because of this low capital requirement, they understood that they could enter the business world and be successful with a pizza parlor. Together, they worked and supplied the necessary ingredients to succeed: hard work, vision and determination. They never wanted to be employees; they wanted to own their own business. This pizza parlor was successful.

The brothers had the vision and understanding of how the demographics of this country had changed. The traditional evening home-cooked meal was disappearing because housewives were now working. The brothers recognized that if they could deliver a delicious and nutritious pizza while it was still hot, there would be a tremendous demand. This was *serendipity*.

Drivers were hired to work on commission and required to deliver the pizzas while they were still hot. The profit for the first weeks was very small, but there was great growth potential. Monaghan deleted special-sized pizzas and sandwiches from his menu and concentrated on delivery of hot pizzas, allowing volume and profits to increase.

The average cost of a medium sized eight-inch is less than $2.00; the major cost is the mozzarella cheese. Average selling price in the Chicago area is approximately $8.00 to $10.00. For a large pizza, with the addition of sausage, pepperoni or other ingredients, the average selling price is around $13.00 to $15.00. The additional ingredients would increase the cost by approximately two to three dollars. The profit margin on pizza is extremely high, and because of that high profitability, Domino's could continue to expand.

The Domino kitchens did not employ chefs. Labor costs were low because the pizza was prepared by semi-skilled people. A formula was established for the preparation of the pizza, which simplified and standardized the preparation process, thereby preserving low labor costs. The finest ingredients were purchased, which created not only a highly nutritious product, but a delicious one as well.

Demand was proven by the continued increase in business. In major cities, the dough is prepared from a central location and delivered to the pizza parlors. This increases the standardization and quality and keeps costs down.

Jim Gilmore, a local chef, helped improve the product and later became a partner.

The formula for the growth of the business was still delivery of hot pizzas. The restaurants that were established were primarily pizza parlors with spaghetti and other simple Italian dishes. Chefs were not employed because they were not necessary. This kept labor costs down.

Franchising was established in 1967 and franchisees were required to keep the Domino's name and continue buying high-quality ingredients. They were supervised periodically to maintain quality control and as a result, profits from these franchises began to float upward. Due to the strong demand of its fine product, advertising and marketing was limited. Domino's continued to expand its store and franchise operations. The partners were highly qualified and continued to manage their operations, not requiring professional management until many years later. Facing the tough competition of Pizza Hut, Domino's makes its first delivery guarantee, "A half hour or a half dollar off." This was later abandoned because of the carelessness of delivery drivers. However, delivery of hot pizza still continued.

To decentralize the management, regional offices were established in six cities to oversee 500 stores and in 1983, in Winnipeg, Manitoba, Canada, Domino's first international store opened and followed with stores as far away as Israel and Australia. Growth continued nationally and internationally. Because of the demand, sales increased to approximately $1 million and by 1998 increased to approximately $2 million. By 2001, net income grew from $25 million to approximately $37 million on sales of $1.3 billion.

The first public offering of Domino's on the New York Stock Exchange occurred in July of 2004. It was widely accepted and the investors proved to have made a good investment. All of this has made Domino's an internationally acclaimed company, all based on a simple, highly nutritious and tasty pizza.

KEY FACTS

1. Start-up capital was $500, augmented by the partners' vision, hard work and desire to be employers, not employees.

2. The American public has a great demand for pizza, a delicious and highly nutritious food.

3. Sit-down restaurants had limited menus, which did not require skilled chefs.

4. The partners recognized that the traditional home-cooked meal was disappearing because many mothers had returned to work. Delivering

a nutritious, delicious pizza while it was still hot could fulfill this need. (*serendipity*)

5. Decentralized centers provided strict supervision over the franchisees, thereby maintaining the high quality and reducing costs.

6. Franchising, both nationally and internationally, provided an upstream flow of profit to the parent corporation.

7. Standardization in the production of the product enabled the quality to be maintained and kept costs down.

8. The brothers had great managerial abilities, which included foresight and wisdom. Decentralized management enabled the supervision of the franchisees and various outlets.

KEY LESSONS

1. Start-up capital can be small.

2. The desire to be employers, not employees, is an extremely motivating factor.

3. Partners are an essential ingredient in success.

4. Quality and integrity of the product must be established early on and maintained throughout the life of the business.

5. Supervision of the franchise outlets was continuous and strict in order to maintain integrity.

6. Standardization of production allowed lower labor costs and high quality.

7. The partners were highly capable managers and hired executives to supplement their growing operations.

ELECTRIC TOOTHBRUSH

Inventor George Clemens who developed the electric hand drier used in washrooms, determined that there would be a great demand for an electric toothbrush that could remove plaque from the teeth. He was confident that he had the ability and motivation to invent this new product.

The commonly used handheld toothbrush cannot remove plaque, the reason for most gum disease and tooth decay. However, an electric toothbrush could do so. An increase in instances of gum disease in a population with rising longevity created demand for such a product. In 1970, Clemens, working in his basement, started to develop the electric toothbrush. Material such as batteries and brushes were available—all he had to do was combine them into a workable prototype.

Developing a new manufacturing product is a long and expensive process, with the final results still to be determined. Robert Merriam and partners invested a moderate amount. Probably less than $1 million in capital was needed for research and development.

The flexibility of fibers used in the tufts of manual toothbrushes dissipates energy, limiting their ability to clean well. To be effective, power imparted to the fiber tufts needs to be transmitted to the surface of the tooth so that the tufts can scrub plaque away.

Clemens' long search for fiber tufts that were stiff enough to transmit cleaning power, but soft enough so they did not abrade the gums and other soft tissues, ended while he was sailing. While on the boat, Clemens made the important discovery that rope became stiff when twisted and then relaxed and soft when untwisted. This would enable the newly designed bristles to remove plaque from teeth without damage to the teeth or the gums.

This discovery by Clemens of the twisting and untwisting of a rope can be recognized by anyone who has ever twisted the end of a thread to push it through the eye of a needle. It is common for entrepreneurs to suddenly have an unforeseen and extremely beneficial event solve the problem, and then proceed with the development of the product: *serendipity*.

Experimenting, tinkering and inventing, George found that rotating the tufts constantly in one direction did not work because torque makes the tufts run out. To create twisting without uncontrollable torque, he decided that the tufts had to oscillate back and forth. He mounted each tuft on a separate gear and had a ratchet move rapidly back and forth to impel the gears to twirl the tufts first in one direction and then the other.

Clemens contacted Leo Shapiro, founder of Leo Shapiro & Associates, a highly respected national and international market research firm, to assist in the marketing of the product. Shapiro took as his fee a percentage of the royalties. Market research proved that there would be a great demand for an electric toothbrush that was reliable and could remove plaque. The study included public awareness of plaque and its dangers. Despite informed awareness, people were still unwilling and not very motivated to brush as long as necessary to remove the plaque with a manual brush, as this required at least two minutes of brushing, followed by flossing, twice a day.

The toothbrushes were given to dentists for testing, and the electric toothbrush was proven to be a reliable and successful product. Adults and children with gum diseases were going to endodontists, and would pay for whatever recommendations were made.

The concept tests demonstrated that if the product was offered at under $150, there would be sufficient demand to produce the toothbrush in quantity. The Interplak team would share 40-50% of the retail profits with the dentists for recommending their product. The marketing costs were astronomical, requiring an initial selling price of $130. Further research found that producing the product in large quantities could bring costs down to $10-12 per toothbrush.

The American Dental Association subsequently approved the product. Contact was made with Gillette, Upjohn and others, who showed little or no interest. INTERPLAK'S patents were due to expire in two years. Subsequently, Gillette's engineering staff was able to work around the patents and introduced an electric toothbrush called the Oral B. It was a reliable and successful product. Clemens' failure was to continue improving his product and neglecting to obtain additional patents.

The group sold the brush (lock, stock and patent) to a group with the financial capabilities and the will to bring it to market. After further development, the electric toothbrush was introduced under the name INTERPLAK. It was immediately successful and Clemens continued to receive royalties.

*Much of this material was created from the pre-publication volume of *What We Learned on Earth* by Leo J. Shapiro and Erik A. Shapiro. Leo Shapiro & Associates is based in Chicago. Leo Shapiro is the chairman and George Rosenbaum is president.

KEY FACTS

1. George Clemens had invented the highly successful hand drier and saw there would be a great demand for an electric toothbrush, which could remove plaque. The new product was developed in his basement with many of the components already available.

2. The bristles presented a problem, which was solved by his ability, while sailing, to notice how the ropes twisted and turned. This application was used to solve the brush problems. (*serendipity*)

3. Robert Merriam and partners recognized that Clemens could develop the toothbrush and invested approximately $1 million.

4. Developing a new manufacturing product is always a long and expensive process, with the final results still to be determined.

5.   Clemens went to approximately thirty-five major companies, including pharmaceutical companies, who showed no interest. They were not interested in financing entrepreneurs.

6.   Clemens' failure to obtain additional patents allowed competitors to work around his patents and create successful competing electric toothbrushes, such as Oral B.

7.   Major corporations are not interested in financing the development of products by entrepreneurs and will purchase only a finished product. Or a major corporation could take an entrepreneur's product, which could end up as a lesser product among the corporation's existing line. The entrepreneur does not need major corporations. He or she can market and sell the product independently.

KEY LESSONS

1.   A proven success will encourage investors.

2.   Developing a new manufacturing process is open-ended as to time, and cost and the product's ultimate reliability and consumer acceptance can remain questionable for quite some time. To accommodate time, costs and provide resources, outside investors are frequently necessary.

3.   The final product must not only be reliable to meet the demand, it must also show low production costs and a high profitability.

4.   Competitors will attempt to create similar products while obtaining their patents in going around the inventor's patents. The inventor must continue to obtain new patents in order to protect the initial product.

5.   Investors will require proof of the demand. This can be accomplished through a reliable market research firm.

6.   Entrepreneurs must be confident and highly motivated in order to succeed.

PASTE-ON FINGERNAILS

My brother's neighbor, Herman Goldenberg, and his brother Leo were the inventors of the <u>paste-on fingernails.</u> Leo was employed by a company producing hair dyes for women. The brothers both wanted to leave their current employment and become self-employed. The capital requirements were low. They recognized that there would be a great demand for this product, since women historically have an interest in cosmetics.

Do-it-yourself paste-on fingernails were the main resource used by women. This was a messy method, which frequently failed. Approval by the Federal Drug Administration was obtained, and the product was patented and marketed through licensing of the patent as well as extensive late-night television advertising. Additional patents were obtained to protect the original patent.

They were among the early users of the frequently packaged product advertised on television selling for $19.95 plus handling and delivery charges. [? Perhaps: The Goldenberg's were one of the first advertisers marketing their product via late-night television ads.] The original paste-on fingernails were sold for approximately $14.95 plus shipping and handling. The manufacturing cost was approximately $1.00 as the paste-on fingernails could be mass-produced.

The use of the paste-on fingernails also became commonly used on women's toes. The selling price of the product through the drugstores and cosmetic shops was approximately $7.00 to $8.00 for the fingernails and somewhat higher for the pedicure nails. There was a great demand for this beautifying product. High quality standards were established and always maintained.

Initial capital required was probably in the vicinity of $25,000. Additional costs were incurred because it had to be approved by the Federal Drug Administration and attorneys were retained for this purpose. The total cost was probably less than $100,000. Both brothers became wealthy.

KEY FACTS

1. There is always a demand, especially among women, for quality cosmetic products. Paste-On Fingernails fulfilled the great demand at a relatively low cost.

2. Initial capital was $25,000. Federal Drug Administration approval was necessary, which necessitated attorney's fees. Additional patents were also obtained. The total capital was increased to $100,000.

3. Marketing was primarily through late-night television spot ads. Retail drugstores were also a source for sales. Retail price was approximately $8.00 for fingernails and somewhat higher for pedicure nails. Licensing of the patents also provided an upward stream of profit.

4. Because of extremely high profit and great demand, outside capital was never required.

5. Both brothers became wealthy.

6. Integrity of the product was always maintained.

7. The manufacturing process was outsourced, enabling the brothers to direct their energies towards the quality of the product and marketing.

KEY LESSONS

1. Demand for a beautifying product for women was easily recognized.

2. The total capital of $100,000 was provided by the two brothers. Because of the demand and profitability of the product, outside investors were not sought.

3. Because of the great demand, spot TV ads and sales through drugstores was sufficient. The manufacturing process provided a reliable and low-cost product.

4. The brothers possessed great managerial skills and kept their focus on their proven and reliable product.

5. The brothers were highly motivated, skillful and confident of success.

6. One brother resigned his executive position at a corporation and together they formed a partnership, enabling them to be employers, not employees.

VELCRO

In 1941, George de Mestral was hiking through the Alpine countryside walking his dog, where cockleburs continually fastened themselves to his trouser legs. He examined the burs under a microscope to discover why they fastened themselves to fabrics. He was curious. What had nature created over a period of millions of years that would attach itself to clothing? He was confident that he could develop a product and became a businessman. He had the time and energy to pursue his curiosity. It took de Mestral eight years of tinkering to develop a usable product made out of nylon hooks and loops. The main challenge was perfecting the manufacturing process to ensure consistent results. He had invented a highly reliable and useful product for which he recognized there would be a great demand. This was *serendipity*.

VELCRO was name of this new product. The word is a combination of two French words for velvet and hook: "velour" and "crochet." The early years were a struggle. Fortunately, the only capital required was brainpower, motivation, curiosity and the continued search for the answer to what nature had developed. Eventually, Mestral entered into an agreement with Jean Revaud, who acquired the rights to his product. De Mestral became a millionaire.

The manufacturing process produces a low cost, high-quality product, which can be produced in large quantities. Patents were obtained both nationally and internationally to protect the product. Additional patents were obtained to protect the original patent. The selling price of this product in its many forms created huge profits, which enabled the company to expand internationally. The usefulness of this product has increased tremendously. Velcro is used to fasten diapers, sleeping suits of astronauts, purses, shoes, baseball gloves and thousands of products. It is so commonplace that people take the product for granted.

KEY FACTS

1. George de Mestral, a keen observer and tinkerer, developed this highly reliable and useful product at home. Initial capital was approximately $2,000.

2. What had nature developed over millions of years that man could duplicate? His observations of the cocklebur led to his invention of Velcro: *serendipity*.

3. He was curious, skillful and determined. It took eight years of tinkering to develop the product.

4. He recognized immediately that there would be a great demand for this very reliable product. Manufacturing provided a reliable low-cost product that had great margins of profit.

5. Mr. de Mestral sold all of his rights to a major corporation, became a millionaire and retired.

6. Being curious and observant can lead you to a niche in becoming an entrepreneur.

7. Patents are granted to protect the invention because competitors could possibly engineer around the original patent. Additional patents should be obtained.

KEY LESSONS

1. Requirements: being critical, observant, confident and determined.

2. Demand for the product must be recognized immediately by the entrepreneur.

3. Because of the great demand for this reliable product, extensive marketing was not necessary.

4. The inventor, entrepreneur, did not wish to continue in the management and sold all rights and was able to retire at an early age.

5. Additional patents should be obtained in order to prevent competitors from obtaining other patents to produce a similar product.

KINKO'S

In 1970, Paul Orfalea graduated from college in Isla Vista, California, near Santa Barbara. He rented a small store to produce copies. He named the store after his nickname, "Kinko," which his friends called him because of his red, kinky hair.

What this entrepreneur recognized was that there was great demand for simple, clean, low-cost copies, because not everyone had access to an office copy machine. He also envisioned that Kinko's could be an office away from home, not only for business people, but also for any person that needed work done.

The start-up capital required was less than $5,000 for rent, utilities and supplies. He leased the copy equipment, thereby preserving his capital. "Kinko" wanted to be an entrepreneur and his own boss. He had the required initial capital, confidence and perseverance to open his Kinko's shop.

The customers were taught to make copies on simple copy machines. Staffing was by well-trained, pleasant employees who were there to teach the customers how to make their own copies. The principal cost, the paper, was negligible. As photocopiers continued to evolve and improve, customers were able to get photocopies of increasingly high quality at a very low price. Demand was rising. Because of high profitability and low cost, expansion could be increased without the infusion of outside capital.

Kinko's grew and began to offer posters and large copies, color copies and business cards. Auxiliary items, such as stationery and school and office supplies, were offered and provided an additional source of income. The offices were strategically located near colleges and near or outside office areas. Many stores were open twenty-four hours. Faxing services also became a highly profitable source of revenue.

Kinko's continued to expand and has approximately 26,000 employees worldwide. Since its inception, the company has enjoyed a reputation for quality, speed and service. In 2005, Federal Express purchased Kinko's for $2.5 billion cash.

KEY FACTS

1. Paul Orfalea, "Kinko," just out of college, realized there would be a great demand for an inexpensive photocopying shop.

2. "Kinko" became the employer and was never an employee.

3. Initial capital was $5,000. High demand and profitability resulted in excellent revenue streams and expansion was accomplished without having to raise outside capital.

4. The stores were strategically placed near college campuses and office buildings and staffed by highly trained, respectful and helpful employees. Being able to purchase stock made the employees more dedicated to the prosperity of the company.

5. Highly reliable and useful machines were leased, preserving capital for future expansion. Customers were taught to make their own copies and assistance was available.

6. Wall Street subsequently recognized this highly profitable business and infused capital.

7. Kinko's became an international company, providing an office away from home throughout the world.

FedEx recognized that Kinko's would supplement its on-going business by combining office and shipping services and purchased Kinko's in 2005.

KEY LESSONS

1. Demand can be easily recognized by the entrepreneur simply by providing a service that mirrors his or her own needs.

2. The expensive copying equipment was leased, thereby preserving capital and substantially reducing start-up costs.

3. "Kinko" proved he had the necessary management skills to create an international company. The focus always remained on providing a way for customers to make do-it-yourself photocopies.

4. Teaching the customer to make their own copies substantially reduced labor costs. Staff assistance was readily available.

5. The stores, many open twenty-four hours, provided the consumer with an office away from the office or home.

6. Businesses recognized that the speedy, highly reliable and low-cost products were an important complement to their business.

XEROX CORPORATION

In 1938, patent attorney Chester Carlson invented the first xerography image. Up to that time, duplicate copies were made with the use of carbon paper, a labor intensive and difficult method of making duplicate. A photographic process was later introduced which was messy, expensive and unreliable. Perhaps one of three copies was acceptable.

Carlson patented his electro photography process (later renamed xerography) having recognized there would be great demand for a process to create reliable, speedy and low-cost copies. He had the skills, motivation and perseverance necessary to succeed. Also, he would not have to be an employee, but could run his own company.

In 1947, he recognized the need for a partner to provide additional capital to develop the process. The partner was Haloid, a small photo-paper maker. It is estimated that the capital requirement from the initial inception to the development of the product was approximately $1 million. The Haloid Company recognized the potential of this process and would also require using paper. It was a sound and profitable investment.

The development of a manufacturing process is costly, time consuming and the final product still to be proven. Xerox, ultimately the new name of the company, introduced the first quality product, the Model A, in 1949. The new product was simple to use and fulfilled the great demand that existed. It was a phenomenal success. Patents, both nationally and internationally were obtained. Over the years, additional patents were obtained to protect the original patent and subsequent improvements to the product. All previous methods of copying had become virtually obsolete.

There was great growth in the sale of Xerox copy machines, with ten thousand copiers sold in 1962, and revenues of approximately $23 million. Research and development continued, which resulted in the introduction of many useful, low cost and highly reliable products. These products enabled greater operating efficiency in offices and in general public use. The word "Xerox" itself became a verb, and copy machines have been a fixture in offices around the world ever since.

KEY FACTS

1. Carlson, an inventor, recognized there would be a great demand for a simpler method of creating documents.

2. He had the experience, determination and confidence to succeed.

3. He recognized that he did not have the resources to develop the manufacturing process. He first formed a partnership with Battell Memorial

Institute, which later worked with Haloid to develop the Xerox machine. It is estimated the approximately one million dollars was necessary.

4. The great public demand for this reliable product reduced the need for extensive marketing.

5. The company continued to grow and supply useful and reliable products through the establishment of research centers.

6. A New Jersey businessman by the name of "Leavitt" also recognized the future of xerography and brought in a large infusion of capital.

KEY LESSONS

1. Entrepreneurs must recognize the demand for a new product and have the motivation, skills and confidence to proceed. Be alert to *serendipity*!

2. Required additional capital can be supplied from outside sources once the investor recognizes the potential demand for the product.

3. Developing a manufacturing process is open ended. It requires undetermined capital investment, time and questions as to the reliability of the final product. Partnerships are usually required for the additional necessities.

4. Because of the great demand and profitability, Wall Street eventually was necessary for the capital to make Xerox an international company.

5. Focus has always remained on this low cost, highly profitable and reliable product. Even with the addition of other products, photocopying has remained its core business.

6. Ultimately the product had to be available at low cost, for if cost is too high, demand will diminish.

7. A successful invention will create competition. The inventor's patent is meant to protect the invention for a limited time. Smart competitors, engineers, will attempt to go around the patent to develop a competing product.

MICROSOFT

Bill Gates, age nineteen, a student at Harvard University, and his lifelong friend, Paul Allen, twenty-one, were both extremely knowledgeable in the use of computers, had experience and insight into the need for software for the operation of computers. One day, while visiting Gates in his dorm room, Allen brought along a copy of the magazine, Popular Electronics. The cover featured a picture of the Altair 8080, with a headline exclaiming "World's First Microcomputer Kit to Rival Commercial Models." Gates and Allen instantly realized that home computers were about to burst on the marketplace, and they recognized that someone was going to need to write the software for these computers. Gates contacted the company that made the Altair, Micro Instrumentation and Telemetry Systems, and within eight weeks Gates and Allen delivered program software to MITS. The company bought the rights to their BASIC program, and both young men realized that the market for software was just beginning. By year-end, Gates dropped out of Harvard and together, Gates and Allen formed Microsoft, in 1975. The only capital required was motivation, brainpower, curiosity and diligence. Gates and Allen were confident that they could succeed and founded their own company. They had found a niche in the computer world for which they realized there would be a great demand.

The growth of Microsoft is a legend that has not had to be retold. Microsoft's BASIC product continued to develop and was now being leased to and used by major national and worldwide companies.

Microsoft hired talented, experienced employees, who formed teams where ideas could be exchanged, which assisted in the growth of the company. Engineers were later employed for the same purpose. The two groups supplemented one another.

Microsoft became a giant corporation with centralized management. New executives were hired from outside sources and there were promotions within the company. Apple computers, Radio Shack, Sirius, Zenith, Sharp and other companies licensed the Microsoft products. Headquarters were established in Bellevue, Washington.

Great growth continued through the development of innovative and user-friendly products. Integrity of Microsoft products has been a cornerstone of its success.

Bill Gates was president and Paul Allen was executive vice president. Manufacturing and distribution for Europe was established in Ireland. 1986 was the first public offering at $21 per share and increased to $28 per share by the end of the day. Capital raised was $61 million. By 1987 the share value was approximately $85 per share and Bill Gates became a billionaire at age thirty-one.

Ninety percent of all computers throughout the world use Microsoft systems. It was also used in over 200 countries and in 39 languages. Competitors arose but Microsoft still dominated. Revenue increased to tens of billions of dollars per year.

KEY FACTS

1. Young and inspired and with a great deal of serendipitous awareness of a burgeoning home computer market, Gates and Allen developed software to fulfill an up and coming demand.

2. The only capital was curiosity, brainpower and motivation to succeed and be their own bosses.

3. The demand for their reliable and useful products was high from its inception.

4. Licensing agreements with users provided an upward stream of cash. The licenses were always owned by Microsoft, which also gave them control of their product.

5. Because of the strong demand, marketing and advertising were limited.

6. Management continued primarily under Gates. Additional executives were promoted from within the company or from outside sources.

7. A headquarters was established in Bellevue, WA. Continued research and development of new products that were useful and reliable was supplemented by a staff of young computer scientists and engineers. This enabled Microsoft to maintain its leadership position over all competitors.

KEY LESSONS

1. Partners can provide insight, motivation, skills and support.

2. Outside capital was not required. The licensing agreements and their profitability provided sufficient capital for growth.

3. Their insights and skills led them to recognize a great demand for programs for the computer industry.

4. One partner had outstanding managerial skills. Support for growth was through promotion or the hiring of skilled computer specialists and engineers.

HEWLETT PACKARD

William Hewlett and David Packard, engineering graduates of Stanford University, became partners in 1939. They combined their knowledge, insights and motivation and started working to produce equipment which they felt was in demand in the emerging field of electronics. With capital of just over $500, and a used drill press, they began to develop equipment in Packard's garage. As with all entrepreneurs, they were confident they could succeed.

The first successful product was called a resistance-capacity audio oscillator, used to test sound equipment. Walt Disney became their first big customer by ordering eight HP-200Bs for the animated production of *Fantasia*.

Hewlett-Packard, Inc. was incorporated in 1947. The revenues were approximately $700,000. Additional electronic products were developed for which there was great demand, including a high-speed frequency counter. Radio and FM stations recognized a need for this reliable product. There was a substantial increase in revenues, as the company's highly reliable products were in great demand. Revenues reached approximately $5.5 million.

Hewlett and Packard recognized that existing computers were large, cumbersome and slow, and in many instances required air conditioners for cooling. They developed the first PC in 1968. It was revolutionary. There was great demand for this superb computer. It had great computing capacity, reliability, speed and low cost and was a tremendous success.

In 1957, a public stock offering was made and widely accepted. By 1965, revenues were approximately $165 million.

In order to continue to grow and meet continuing market demand, a large research and development facility was established where knowledgeable computer scientists and engineers were employed. Many reliable products were introduced into the marketplace.

The first hand-held calculator replaced the slide rule in 1972. HP entered into the business computer market in competition with IBM and Digital Equipment Corporation in 1972. HP products were highly accepted by the market.

In 1974, several divisions were established, allowing each division to conduct research and development independently. In the same year, revenues were $3 billion. Fortune magazine ranked HP 49th among its 500 companies, with sales of approximately $9 billion in 1988.

KEY FACTS

1. Hewlett and Packard, both highly trained engineers, began working in their garage, developing products to fulfill the need for the fledgling electronics industry. The total capital required was little more than $500.

2. They were both highly motivated, confident and did not want to become employees of any company.

3. Integrity of their useful products was established at the inception and continued throughout its history. Advertising and marketing was limited because of the great demand and reliability of this useful product.

4. Research and development facilities were established under the direction and control of Hewlett and Packard. This ensured a steady flow of useful and reliable products to meet the demand for this growing electronics industry. Both men also had outstanding managerial abilities.

5. HP recognized that a small home computer with capacity, speed and low cost was necessary. They developed the first personal computer.

6. Walt Disney purchased their first product, which gave HP industry-wide recognition.

7. High profitability of the products provided the necessary capital for expansion without the need of great infusion of capital from other financial resources.

KEY LESSONS

1. The partners combined knowledge, experience and motivation, which allowed them to become entrepreneurs with only a small amount of capital required.

2. Combining their knowledge and insights gave them the ability to perceive there would be a demand for testing equipment.

3. Because of the useful, reliable and easy-to-use products, the company became international.

4. The founders always maintained a very high degree of control in research and management.

GOOGLE

In 1995, Larry Page and Sergei Brin, both Stanford University computer science graduate students, still in their twenties, recognized there would be great demand for a search engine that could be a single source for researching the information that exists on the Internet.

The total initial capital was their brainpower and personal computers. They were knowledgeable, highly motivated and confident of their potential success. Young, curious, eager, confident and smart, they developed a computer application that allows users to sift through the largest data set in the world, the Internet. Why should people have such difficulty finding sources of information?—they asked themselves. They liked the idea of being their own bosses, and set out to devise a solution.

By having all the information in their retrieval system, originally called Backrub, Page and Brin examined the underlying links that point to any given Web site. The two realized that an analytical search engine—one that sorted sites by the number of links attached to it—would provide a reliable, broad source of information for which there would be a great demand for both individual and corporate users.

In 1997, Page and Brin registered the domain name "google.com" and began searching for financial partners and/or licensees. After failing to find major corporations interested in their technology, they developed a business plan. They named their search engine technology "Google," an offshoot of the word googol, which is the number one followed by 100 zeros.

In 1998, PC Magazine named Google among its "Top 100 Web Sites and Search Engines." Andy Bechtolsheim of Sun Microsystems, invested $100,000 in the company in 1998. This was the first infusion of capital. Up to this point, the capital investment of the two partners was less than $10,000. They became incorporated under "Google, Inc." with the two partners as principal shareholders. Inquiries reached 10,000 a day.

In 1999, headquarters were established in Menlo Park, California with only eight employees. Inquiries per day grew to 500,000. A major investment of $25 million was made by Sequoia Capital and Kleiner, Perkins, Caulfield & Buyers. New headquarters were established and dubbed the Googleplex in Mountain View, California.

Not only were employees given the opportunity to have time for playing street hockey in the parking lot, they were also permitted to purchase stock.

Inquiries reached three million per day when AOL and Netscape decided to feature Google as their search engine of choice. Time magazine named Google one of its "Top Ten Best Cybertech" companies. Google became available in ten languages.

A one-billion-page index was developed in 2000 and search queries per day grew to eighteen million, the company became the largest search engine in the world and was also introduced in Asian languages. Asian countries also began using Google in their own languages.

To the user, Google was and remains free. The advertisers paid Google to feature their product or service. In 2000, Google split fees it received from advertisers with the Web site owners. It was a highly profitable product and always remained a most reliable and useful search engine, recognized throughout the world.

Dr. Erik Schmidt became chairman and the company was divided with Page as president of Product Development and Brin as president of Technology Development. Google continued to expand with national and international sites. Offices opened in Tokyo, Japan, and Hamburg, Germany.

Profits for the year 2003 totaled approximately $105 million on sales of $962 million. In 2004, a Dutch auction was offered with stocks selling at $85 per share, which increased to 4,100 per share by the end of the day. More than twenty-two million shares had been traded. Page and Brin both became multi-billionaires at a very early age.

KEY FACTS

1. Page and Brin recognized that there would be a demand for a new and simple method of searching for information.

2. While graduate students, with the use of their computers, they developed a search engine for the Internet, which was easy to use and highly reliable. Their capital was their combined knowledge, insights, and motivation, desire to be their own boss and approximately $5,000.

3. Sun Microsystems recognized the great demand for a product that Page and Brin had developed and the quality of their product and invested $100,000.

4. The product also had potential for high profitability.

5. Marketing came naturally through the recognition that Google was a most useful search product. Advertising was not necessary.

KEY LESSONS

1. Partners can bring together knowledge, insights, motivation and support.

2. Their combined abilities led them to recognize there was a great need for their software.

3. It was free to the user. The advertisers paid to show their products.

eBAY

In 1995, the idea for eBay.com was born during conversations between founder Pierre Omidyar and his wife, an avid Pez collector who had difficulty finding other collectors with whom she could trade. Omidyar formed a sole proprietorship and conducted an online auction under the name Auction Web. It was later incorporated in the state of Delaware. Fees were charged starting in 1996. The company was renamed eBay in 1997.

eBay served the role of broker. They did not own any of the items being sold and were not responsible for collection or distribution. Bidding was free, but it did cost between 25 cents and $2 to list an item for sale, plus a commission of between 2.5 and 5 percent of the sale price. The site was profitable almost from the beginning, unlike the vast majority of e-commerce sites. Recognizing there would be a great demand for an on-line auction house, since many buyers and sellers of products could not meet to transact business, eBay became the source.

Capital required by Omidyar was negligible, since the transactions were done online, with fees being paid by the seller. Public demand for this useful, easy and inexpensive way to sell and buy products grew quickly. Approximately $5.8 million in fees was generated during the first year of operation. By 1998, gross merchandise sales were approximately $100 million and revenues were $6 million. This reflected tremendous growth. Because of the fees paid by the users, capital requirements were limited.

The first public offering was at NASDAQ in 1998. The value of the stock increased tremendously. In 2001, sales were $750 million and profits were approximately $140 million. Great growth continued because of the demand for this useful auction process. In 1998, the eBay Foundation was established with the contribution of approximately 108,000 shares of eBay common stock to Community Foundation Silicon Valley (CFSV). The purpose was to provide philanthropy and build a stronger community.

In order to reduce the incidence of fraud, a feedback rating system was introduced. The buyers and sellers were notified of the rating system. The higher the positive feedback number, the more reliable the company or the seller. Negative ratings were also established to warn users of potential problems. A seller with a rating of-4 was denied the use of eBay services.

Local online auction houses were established to sell automobiles and even real estate. Meg Whitman, a CEO from Hasbro, Inc. became the CEO and Pierre Omidyar became chairman. Both Omidyar and his wife were now multi-millionaires.

The use of eBay grew phenomenally with the number of registered users climbing to ten million. E-bay offers over 3,000 product categories and lists more than three million items for sale.

KEY FACTS

1. Pierre Omidyar and his wife recognized that the Internet was a fertile ground for a buyers and sellers of a product to do business and created eBay.

2. eBay became very profitable since operating costs were low; its only major cost was the method by which the buyer and seller were brought together on the Internet.

3. The seller paid a fee to eBay for use of its services.

4. Initial capital was less than $10,000. The sellers provided a constant flow of profit.

5. Fraud was a problem, which was virtually eliminated by the establishment of a rating system. eBay acts as the broker, having no financial interest in either the buyer or the seller.

6. Marketing was accomplished through the acknowledgement by the general public that eBay was a simple, quick, reliable, economical and even fun way to buy and sell.

7. By recognizing the need for which there is a great demand and supplying the method, the founders became multi-millionaires.

KEY LESSONS

1. A simple need of his wife's gave the founder insights to start this giant company, and is a good example of serendipity.

2. His knowledge of the possibilities of the Internet led him to develop the software that fulfilled the great demand.

3. The product was extremely profitable because the sellers paid the fees. It was free to the buyer.

4. The operating costs were merely the programs owned by the founder.

5. Competition arose, but the sound management by the founder continued, enabling continued growth.

AMERICAN RARITIES COINS

Robert Lalas, the only son of my longtime secretary, Jan Lalas, was a rare coin hobbyist. While in college, he worked at Kmart and McDonald's, but he did not intend to continue on as an employee. At a convention center, sponsored by the local coin club and held in Springfield IL, collectors could rent a table for $20. A bourse was opened where others could sell or exchange coins, baseball cards and similar items. He rented a table and made approximately $100 at this first bourse. He realized this was going to be his future. It was profitable, an area in which he enjoyed working and he could be his own boss.

His initial capital of $10,000 was provided by his parents to open a coin shop in Burbank, IL, a south suburb of Chicago, in 1988. It was moderately success-ful. His great breakthrough (serendipity) came through the use of the Internet approximately nine years later. A fellow coin collector told him about the Internet and Robert thought it was worthwhile trying. This enabled him to trade and sell coins on a countrywide basis.

His total business volume is approximately $700,000 to $1,000,000 per year. This provides Robert with an upper middle class standard of living. He owns his home in a southern suburb, where he lives with his wife and three children. He never expected to become a multimillionaire and is comfortable with his accom-plishments and status in life.

KEY FACTS

1. Robert discovered early on he wanted to be self-employed. He had worked for Kmart and McDonalds and realized this was not to be his future.

2. He was highly motivated and experienced in the collection of coins.

3. His hobby gave him the knowledge and direction to pursue his future life.

4. The local coin club provided him an avenue through a bourse, where he made $100 at the first meeting.

5. Initial capital of $10,000 was provided by his parents.

6. He did not need a partner, since he already was very knowledgeable in the buying and selling of coins. A partner could not have added anything to his business.

7. Curiosity as to the benefits of using the Internet led him to expand his business nationally.

KEY LESSONS

1. A hobby can lead an entrepreneur into his or her future.

2. Consumers recognized they were able to buy, sell or exchange coins through a reliable source. The demand for a reliable product has to be recognized and developed.

3. Capital requirements are often low for entrepreneurs.

4. Great growth resulted from use of the Internet.

5. Robert was able to achieve a highly desirable and satisfying lifestyle through his business.

PETERSEN REALTY COMPANY, CHICAGO

Len Petersen has been my friend and client since approximately 1956. When he returned from India, where he served in the Second World War, he told me that he did not know where his future lay. This was common feeling among returning veterans, many of who were young and had not yet begun their professional careers.

His brother, Bud, was already employed by Saleson Realty Company on North Avenue in Chicago. Lenny told me that he felt very comfortable with numbers and details. He liked working with people and was a hard worker. Len consequently found his future in real estate and joined his brother at Saleson Realty. He was surprised and pleased at his early successes and was soon promoted to manager.

After several years, Len obtained a real estate broker's license and founded Petersen Realty Company on the 4400 block of Fullerton Avenue in Chicago. Fullerton is a major east/west street. The area had many homes and some apartment buildings. His early salespeople consisted of Bud and his mother, Irma, who happened to be a superb real estate salesperson.

The savings that he had from being a salesperson was approximately $10,000, sufficient capital for his new office. He explained that all one really needed for a real estate office was desks, telephones, utilities and a part-time secretary. Funds are also required to advertise and receive real estate listings, but other than that is business relatively free of overhead.

Real estate salespeople are not employees, they are a independent contractors. The broker who hires salespeople does not have to provide insurance coverage or pay social security and other benefits. These are the expenses in a normal business, but real estate is different inasmuch as the sale listings are the business' inventory.

Len worked eight to ten hours a day and loved it. His office was successful and the income provided him with a very nice middle-class standard of living. He never was ambitious to become a multi-millionaire. Being a successful real estate broker was a wonderful way to go.

Len was my first real estate client and he introduced me to other brokers. This enabled me to become a specialist as a real estate lawyer. Being an attorney in real estate is a transaction business where everyone comes out happy. The seller comes out with cash, the buyer with a home, and the broker/salesperson with commission and the attorney with fees. The entire transaction from the inception of the real estate contract to the closing is approximately six months.

KEY FACTS

1. Returning from his war service in the Pacific, Len discovered that his brother Bud was already a successful real estate salesman and the business appealed to him.

2. To be a successful real estate salesman, you have to have the ability to work with numbers and be comfortable with people. Len had both qualities.

3. He had early successes as a salesman for Saleson Realty in Chicago, which gave him the sweet taste for his future.

4. He established a small broker's office on the North side of Chicago, with a capital of approximately $10,000. It was a successful venture.

5. A real estate broker provides the desks, telephones and advertising. The real estate salespeople are independent contractors and receive no other benefits except a portion of the fees earned.

6. His office was on a well-known commercial street surrounded by homes and apartment buildings, which were frequently being bought or sold.

7. He never aspired to become a multi-millionaire. He had established a middle class lifestyle to satisfy his immediate needs.

8. He was my first real estate client. We established a personal relationship that has continued for over fifty years.

KEY LESSONS

1. Very little capital is required for a real estate office.

2. High motivation and a love for working with people can enable a broker to establish a high quality, middle class lifestyle.

3. Overhead is low, since only one employee is required (the secretary).

4. Rent and utilities were just the normal expenses of every business.

5. Advertising was the other expense, since in real estate that is the way to sell the product.

6. The salespeople acquired the listings of products to be sold.

7. The broker, in order to finance the sale, established contacts with lenders, primarily in the savings and loan industry.

8. Financing for the buying and selling of home is primarily through banks and savings and loan industry.

9. The broker does not provide the financing for the buyer and seller.

ENTREPRENEURSHIP WITHIN YOUR EMPLOYMENT

If you do not have the resources, motivation or opportunity to become your own boss, there are still ways to benefit from entrepreneurship, even in your current job. Employers are always seeking ways to improve their companies. Employees frequently become aware of a project or idea of value to the employer. If you have an idea that you'd like to propose to your employer, prepare a two-page outline of your plan or idea, emphasizing the following:

A. Potential demand for the new product/idea

B. The cost of production, if it is to be manufactured

C. Potential profitability, and a timeline

Before submitting your proposal, take a precautionary measure to prevent others from stealing or taking credit for the idea themselves. After you have completed your suggestions, send to yourself a registered letter but DO NOT OPEN IT. Sometimes referred to as the "poor man's copyright," the registered letter will have the date and postmark, which proves that it was your idea at that early date.

To give you an idea how valuable the entrepreneurial spirit can be inside a company, consider 3M's Post-It note, one of the most successful products in history. The Post-it note started as an idea that an employee had for using an adhesive 3M had developed that didn't stick very well. The product was not developed through the company's traditional channels, it was the result of effort and faith on the part of a dedicated individual who wanted to see his idea become a reality. He was not paid for this effort, until the product was adopted, after which he was rewarded handsomely.

Extra initiative on the job can pay off in other important ways as well. For example, approximately forty-five years ago, while at my client's bank, the CEO invited me to sit in on an IBM presentation about electric typewriters, which were just being introduced into the market. I learned a great deal from the salesperson's presentation and took his business card. The bank replaced all of their manual typewriters with the new IBM electrics. A few weeks later, I called the IBM salesman to my downtown office to meet with my secretary, and asked him to explain the benefits and uses of the new typewriter. I gave him an order for an electric typewriter that he refused to take. He explained that my office building was not within his sales territory and that he would have the sales representative who covers my office building contact me.

I placed the order with the other salesperson and he said he had never been given an order that quickly. I was very impressed with my initial salesperson and wrote a letter to Tom Watson, president of IBM, expressing my appreciation his outstanding efforts. A short time later, I received a response from Watson thanking me for the correspondence. A carbon copy of my letter was given to the sales manager.

Approximately two weeks later, I received a call from the original IBM salesperson. "Do you know what you did for me?" he said.

I said, "I didn't do anything for you. You did it all by yourself. You took hours away from selling to prospective buyers to help promote and sell the IBM product, for which you have not received any credit. You have demonstrated a devotion to the IBM company, which had to be recognized." I subsequently learned that this person received a well-deserved promotion.

LESSONS TO BE LEARNED

1. Always work to improve the quality and service of your employer.

2. Do so without any expectation of any reward. Recognition will eventually come, one way or another.

3. In this competitive world, always try to perform better than everyone else. This will give you an important edge for advancement and success.

4. When you have an opportunity to compliment an individual for an outstanding job, do so. I always contact the CEO, bypassing the bureaucracy. Likewise, when I have a major complaint that is not being handled well, I contact the CEO, who will always make sure the problem is quickly corrected.

TWO ENTREPRENEURSHIPS THAT FAILED

MOTOROLA—IRIDIUM

Motorola, in Schaumburg, IL, is an international company with a long history of successes. In the early 1960s, the company designed a global satellite mobile phone system, which they recognized would be in great demand. The company devoted more than a decade to research and development of Mobile Satellite Services, which Motorola called Iridium.

In 1996, the Gallup Organization was retained to do an extensive worldwide market research project of this new product. The market research showed that the Iridium business plan had serious flaws. Despite these negative findings, the executives of Motorola proceeded with the launching of the Iridium project, since so much had already been invested in the project. A public offering was made.

In August of 1999, Iridium filed for bankruptcy and thousands of investors lost their money. Motorola had other companies investing in the project. Chase Bank filed a lawsuit against Iridium and Motorola claiming that a loan had been obtained for $300 million just thirty days prior to the filing of the bankruptcy. The company eventually repaid the $300 million. The U.S. Securities and Exchange Commission launched an investigation.

The Iridium Company invested over $5 billion in the Iridium system and it was eventually sold for $25 million, a staggering loss for the investors who purchased the stock and a major loss, both in prestige and funds, for Motorola.

KEY FACTS

1. Research and development for a manufacturing process is expensive and can be expected to take a long time.

2. When the Iridium product was finally manufactured, its quality was questionable.

3. Motorola ignored the negative findings revealed by The Gallup Organization's market research, despite the responsibility that the executives of Motorola owed to the purchasers of the initial stock offering and to the shareholders of Motorola.

4. The executives were of the opinion that there would be a demand for satellite positioning telephone calls. However, the product was so poor that the demand did not materialize.

5. Knowing that the Iridium project had major flaws, Motorola and Wall Street executives should never have made the initial stock offering. They failed to act with integrity in this instance.

6. Since the Iridium project, new technology has moved rapidly ahead and companies have since recognized and met the public's demand to make phone calls throughout the U.S. and the world. New small handheld phones are commonplace. The low cost and product reliability have increased consumer demands for these phones.

KEY LESSONS

1. Manufacturing a new process is expensive, time consuming and the eventual product still has to be proven.

2. Market research is a necessity and executives should not ignore the findings.

3. The CEO and Board of Directors have a fiduciary responsibility to the shareholders and investors.

4. If a product fails to perform with integrity, it should be withdrawn from the market at an early date.

BACH PIANO COMPANY

I founded the Bach Piano Company in 1948 after realizing that there would be a great demand for spinet pianos. Between the Great Depression and the end of the Second World War, piano and/or violin playing had come to a virtual standstill. Yet, prior to the Great Depression, nearly every middle-class home had an upright piano, and playing songs for family and friends was a primary form of entertainment.

After World War II, culture was re-introduced and members of the family began taking musical instruction. The piano was a beautiful piece of furniture and became a centerpiece of living rooms. Because of my own musical background, which began when I started playing the violin at age seven, I knew people would want to provide their children with music education. Piano playing was in great demand by the middle class. The upright pianos were fine instruments, but they were looked upon as old-fashioned instruments because of their size.

Piano manufacturers turned to spinets. The spinets were approximately 40 to 42 inches in height as opposed to upright pianos, which were about 48 to 54 inches high. The spinets were not great musical instruments, but they were adequate. Their size made them popular. Guessing that there would soon be great demand for these pianos, I established a manufacturing plant to cut down "old-fashioned" uprights to spinet size. However, I failed to recognize that this was impossible, for two major reasons, both highly technical. This new spinet was an attractive piece of furniture, but as a piano, it was a terrible product.

If I had had a partner, I believe that he/she might have pointed out that it was impossible, for technical reasons, to cut down pianos. The resulting product was so bad that I repurchased the spinets and returned deposits. The capital requirements were a major part of my father's life savings, which were lost because of this enterprise. Fortunately, years later, with my successful retail piano stores, I was able to repay my father's capital investment.

KEY FACTS

1. Never go into any business that you know nothing about, even if you recognize there would be a demand.

2. In manufacturing, you have the problem of creating the manufacturing equipment and process. Then, you have to determine whether the product that has been created is reliable and will fulfill the demand.

3. The capital required to start a manufacturing business is open-ended because of the two problems of developing the manufacturing process *and* a reliable product.

4. This company was my own individual undertaking. I did not seek any partners, nor did I seek any advice. This was a mistake.

KEY LESSONS

1. In attempting to develop a new manufacturing process, it is important to seek outside advice.

2. The potential demand is not sufficient reason to proceed without first determining whether the process can succeed.

3. Motivation by itself is not sufficient and, without seeking outside advice, can be destructive.

4. Using the author's father's savings was wrong, since I should have recognized the dangers of starting a new manufacturing process.

REVIEW, DISCUSSION AND QUESTIONS

If you were an actual student in my classroom, and have finished the seventeen case studies above, we would now study the key lessons we learned from the successful entrepreneurs:

1. Discover a product for which there will be a demand.
2. A partner can provide support, ideas, criticism, motivation and capital.
3. Start-up businesses, in many instances, have low capital requirements.
4. The product must always have complete integrity.
5. Market research is essential to provide support for investors after they are convinced that you have a reliable product.

LESSONS LEARNED FROM THE TWO FAILURES

1. Always seek advice from reliable outside sources when entering into a new manufacturing process.
2. Developing a new manufacturing process is open-ended as to time and cost, with the question still to be answered: Will the product fulfill the need?
3. When it becomes obvious that the eventual product does not have integrity, it should be withdrawn from the market.
4. The CEO and Board of Directors have a fiduciary responsibility to shareholders and all investors. Failure to act responsibly can result in financial losses and can damage your reputation.

Class, you have now looked through the eyes and into the minds of seventeen businesses developed by entrepreneurs. What are the most important lessons you have learned?

ASSESSING DEMAND (EXAMPLES)

1. Women's desire to become more beautiful using cosmetics. (Paste-On Fingernails)
2. The human need to attach things; staples, paperclips, pins, sewing. (Velcro)

3. Man's desire to own his dwelling place. (Condominiums and Condo Conversions)

HIGHLY SPECIALIZED TRAINING AND BRAIN POWER

1. Microsoft
2. eBay
3. Google
4. Hewlett Packard

THE NEED TO BE YOUR OWN BOSS

1. Starbucks
2. Domino's Pizza
3. American Rarities Coins
4. Petersen Realty Co.
5. Miller Furniture Co.
6. Kinko's

INVENTORS

1. Xerox
2. Electric Toothbrush

TWO THAT FAILED MANUFACTURING

Open-ended as to time and cost, without assurance that the end product will be successful.

1. Motorola-Iridium
2. Bach Piano Co.

NECESSITIES FOR ALL ENTREPRENEURS

1. The ability to perceive a demand that could become the subject for a business.

2. A partner to support, criticize, advise, motivate and to help provide capital.

3. Initial capital is usually low for start-up companies.

4. Great demand and success can only be determined over a period of time.

5. An inquisitive mind coupled with determination, hard work and perseverance are essentials.

6. Support from your spouse can be essential.

7. Investors, at the earlier stages, may not be necessary where there is strong demand and high profitability.

8. Entrepreneurs usually have great management skills, which can be enhanced by the promoting or hiring of people with knowledge of that particular business.

9. Advertising and marketing may not be important because of the great demand for a useful and reliable product.

10. Market research companies can provide the proof of demand that investors will require.

What follows next is a summarization of the key points we gleaned from our examination of the seventeen case studies:

Starbucks

1. A demand for an outstanding cup of coffee.

2. Small amount of start-up capital required.

3. Partners help one another and are essential.

4. Confidence, motivation and desire to be your own boss.

5. Integrity of the product always maintained.

Dominos

1. Recognized that pizza is a tasty and nutritious food for which there is always demand.

2. Partners each supplied capital, labor and motivation to convert a bankrupt pizza parlor into an acceptable and successful pizza place.

3. Established a quality product right from the start.

4. Listened and adopted ideas presented by others.

5. Recognized that the traditional home-cooked meal was virtually disappearing and being able to deliver a hot, tasty and nutritious pizza to fulfill would fill an important demand.

Electric Toothbrush

1. Identified the need to remove plaque by an electric toothbrush.

2. Already a proven inventor with confidence and had the ability to create "Interplak."

3. Used his own home for the development of the product, thereby reducing the need for major capital.

4. Obtained additional capital from a small group of investors when the need arose.

5. Used dentists as a marketing tool.

Paste-On Fingernails

1. Cosmetic products will always be in high demand.

2. The brothers created the paste-on fingernail, which was easy to apply and approved by the government.

3. Start-up capital was small and the product's high profitability meant outside capital wasn't required.

4. The manufacturing process allowed the production of a low-cost, useful and reliable product.

5. Late-night television advertising proved an excellent method of marketing. Later, the paste-on nails were distributed through various retail channels.

Velcro

1. The inventor had an inquisitive mind and was motivated to discover one of nature's secrets.

2. He persevered despite years of trial and error.

3. He recognized there would be great demand for a useful, low-cost and easily produced product.

4. In this case, a partner was not necessary. The inventor could do it all by himself.

Kinko's

1. The desire to fulfill your own needs led "Kinko" to start an office to produce copies.

2. Leased equipment enabled "Kinko" to preserve capital at the inception of the business.

3. He trained the consumer to do the work, and provided assistance from helpful staff when necessary.

4. Extreme profitability enabled expansion without the need for outside capital. Investors will require an interest in your business.

5. "Kinko" was a successful and knowledgeable manager.

Xerox

1. Developing a manufacturing process is a difficult, expensive, long-term process and requires outside capital.

2. Outside investors must be convinced there will be demand for the product.

3. The inventor must have the confidence, motivation and ability to succeed.

4. Haloid invested because it recognized there would be a great potential profit from the development of Xerox. Also, Haloid's main product, paper, would be used.

Microsoft

1. Youth is not encumbered by reasons why things cannot be accomplished.

2. The two partners, highly trained in their field, had the vision to foresee a great demand and the ability to develop the software to fulfill the demand.

3. Brainpower, a computer and a dorm room was all the capital that was necessary.

4. New, easy-to-use products, for which there would be great demand, were developed by young engineers and computer specialists.

5. Outside capital was not necessary for many years because of the great demand and profitability provided by the leasing agreements.

6. The founders, Gates and Allen, were skillful, successful managers and maintained a hands-on management of their company.

Hewlett Packard

1. Young, highly trained partners recognized the great need for development of useful products in the emerging field of testing of electronic equipment.

2. The only initial capital required was brainpower, perseverance, motivation and a garage.

3. The use of their first product by Disney Co. for *Fantasia* proved the integrity and usefulness of their product.

4. Under the management and guidance of the founders, research and development continued with the development of many highly reliable and acceptable products.

5. The existing computers were slow, cumbersome, required air conditioning and, all in all, not an outstanding product.

6. Hewlett and Packard recognized the need for a personal computer, so they developed one.

7. Outside capital will follow where there is a proven demand and a useful, reliable product.

Google

1. Two partners, both in their twenties, graduate students in computer science at Stanford University, recognized the difficulty of obtaining information from the Internet's many sources.

2. The only capital required was their computer, brainpower, their dormitory and the confidence to succeed that comes with youth.

3. Their Internet search engine was able to compile, in one easily usable and reliable source, the many sources of information that exist on the Internet.

4. It was and remains free to the countless users; the revenue source was the advertisers. Example: your television programs are free, but paid for by the advertisers.

eBay

1. Listen to your wife. This author has done so to great benefit, both in life and in business.

2. Omidyar, listening to his wife, recognized the problem of bringing together a buyer and seller.

3. Their business did not require a great deal of capital, because income was generated from fees paid by the seller.

4. Demand for a single source to buy and sell grew quickly, both nationally and internationally.

First Condominium Development Co.

1. As a real estate lawyer with great experience in new condominiums, I recognized that people would rather own than rent their homes.

2. Only a small amount of capital was necessary because we obtained an option with the right to convert from the owner of a small apartment building.

3. Responsibility between the two partners was divided. I did the negotiations, obtained the mortgage financing and appraisal and established the selling prices of the condominium units. My partner was primarily responsible for upgrading the units and the building, and he was responsible for sales.

4. There was constant communication and exchange of ideas between the partners.

5. Each partner was fully informed almost daily of the other's ideas and activities.

6. We recognized the great potential of converting apartment buildings into condominiums throughout the United States.

Motorola-Iridium

1. The size of previous successes is not a guarantee of a future undertaking's success.

2. Motorola, as the leader, recognized that there was a great demand for the ability to make telephone calls from a hand-held telephone to anywhere in the world.

3. Motorola, other corporations and investors, followed with investing over $5 billion into the Iridium project.

4. The ultimate product was of such poor quality that the business failed.

5. The officers and directors knowingly continued in the development after having been warned by market research of the potential failure.

6. There was a failure of integrity of the product and of the officers and directors of Motorola.

Bach Piano Company

1. The exuberance of youth clouded my ability to foresee the great potential for disaster in developing a new product without outside advice and expertise.

2. Manufacturing a new product has many hazards.

3. As with all new manufacturing processes, capital requirements, the timeline and the final products are open-ended.

4. I should have sought outside sources. Using my father's life savings was wrong.

5. *I never gave up on being an entrepreneur*, and through the experience I gained at age 19 in a retail furniture store, I was able to establish retail piano stores and recover my father's savings.

American Rarities Coins

1. A hobby can be developed into a business.

2. The youth, exuberance and motivation to become the boss are amongst the most important ingredients in becoming an entrepreneur.

3. Vision and the opportunity to sell his first coins at the bourse proved to Robert that this was his future.

4. The Internet provided a larger audience for buying and selling coins than previously existed in Robert's small community.

5. Robert developed a happy, middle-class lifestyle and never undertook the pitfalls, dangers and exasperations of trying to become a multi-millionaire.

Miller Furniture Co.

1. I completed one year at a local community college, majoring in accounting. Fortunately, my accounting instructor advised me that I did not have the necessary facility with numbers to become a professional accountant, even though I could do all of the work associated with accounting.

2. I could not receive any direction from my parents in the ways of becoming an entrepreneur in the United States. Both my parents came out of Russian Jewish Orthodox homes. They were immigrants to the U.S. and its opportunities were still foreign to them.

3. Ambitious and always highly motivated, I was determined to succeed. At age 19, I opened a retail furniture store in Chicago. It was moderately successful.

4. Being the sole proprietor in this small retail operation, gave me the necessary lessons I later used in the business world when converting apartment buildings into condominiums and becoming wealthy.

5. Initial capital came from my father, and later was provided through a man who became a mentor of mine.

SECTION II

WELCOME TO THE WIDE, PROFITABLE AND (POTENTIALLY) HAZARDOUS WORLD OF BUSINESS

YOUR BUSINESS AND YOUR BUSINESS PLAN

If you've already determined the business enterprise in which you are going to be an entrepreneur, that's great—but you still don't have a business. You need a BUSINESS PLAN.

I cannot prepare a business plan for you, but I can point you in the right direction and provide you with the essential guidance. The business plan is critical since you will be seeking funds from many sources and each of these sources will require a detailed and accurate explanation of how you plan to proceed, operate and eventually turn a profit. I have used a business plan for many years in order to seek and obtain funds, primarily from banks. But anyone who lends you money will want to want to see your business plan, so creating a thorough, professional-looking document for that purpose is essential.

Under required reading, I have selected a book that will assist you greatly: *The Business Planning Guide* by David H. Bangs (published by Kaplan Business).

Mr. Bangs offers straightforward, simple advice and all the essential information you will need to develop a thorough business plan. The book also contains lots of practical advice on developing and maintaining a healthy business, particularly in the beginning stages.

WHAT TYPE OF BUSINESS

RETAIL, MANUFACTURING, HIGH-TECH OR ONE OF THE OTHER TYPES OF BUSINESS COVERED IN SECTION I?

The nature of your business will determine your financial needs. Retailing will require location, inventory, salesmen, advertising, etc. Manufacturing has different requirements, depending on what you're attempting to produce. Raw materials, processing, packaging, labor and distribution are likely to be part of the package, and if your product sells, you're going to need that accountant again. In any case, once you have selected what type of business you will start, you must think through your financial needs. I highly recommend that you hire an accounting firm that is experienced in setting up business plans. Retaining an experienced accounting firm is essential because they will help you create a document that attracts attention and funding, whereas all laboring alone is likely to do is create lots of work for you, with little or no results to show for it.

OBJECTIVE OF THE BUSINESS PLAN

The business plan is your "road map" to success. Success is a journey, however, so, as with all journeys, you need to follow your map and revise your "route" when necessary. You will need to review your "map" or plan in order to see if you have been sticking to it, and if not, why not? You may also need to revise your plan depending on new ideas, developments and potential problems you encounter along the way.

Following are some questions you are going to have to answer along the way:

WHO ARE THE PRINCIPALS

Every business depends on its executives for wisdom, judgment, experience and guidance. A good executive can improve a company; a bad executive can ruin a company. If your start-up venture only involves you and a partner, you must endeavor to make sound executive decisions until you can hire someone with the experience you need. In any case, make a list of all the principals involved. This list should include:

1. The names of the principals, ages, addresses, phone numbers and email addresses.
2. Everyone's previous business experience in detail (e.g., resume).
3. Educational background, including degrees.

4. The authors of the business plan and the accounting firm with which you have decided to work.

Once the business plan has been completed, you can start looking for funding. But be prepared to answer a lot of questions. For example, a proposed money source is likely to ask you the following questions:

1. What is the purpose of the loan?
2. Is your business a partnership, proprietorship or small corporation?
3. How much money are you requesting?
4. What is the timeline for need and use of funds?
5. What are the probabilities that your business will succeed?
    A. Proof of demand for your product or service.
    B. Demand for a period of several months.
    C. Market research as proof of demand and growth.
    D. Marketing plan and public relations plan.
    E. How has the product been (or is going to be) developed?
    F. Profitability of product.
6. What is the capital investment by the principals?

"Investment" is the key word here, because anyone who puts money into your venture is going to want a reasonable assurance that they are going to see a return on their investment. The financial success of the enterprise will dictate how the investors will be repaid, the timeline for which they can expect repayment, and the extent to which they will benefit, but be aware that the likelihood of return is usually an investor's primary interest. Even if the principals and/or friends and family are the only source of funds, these six questions should still be asked and answered.

NOW PAY ATTENTION CLASS!

To reiterate, I spent many years teaching entrepreneurship at the Business School of the University of Illinois, Chicago, so I will configure this introduction into the business world using the same format I used in my classes. In effect, you, the reader, are my student—but again, because we are not in the same room together, I have structured the following section to approximate the exchange of information and energy in my classrooms, which were always lively.

My students were formed into teams of three or four people, depending on the class size. I would supply them with the essential facts for establishing a real estate business. Each member of the team was required to purchase a copy of the book I recommended earlier, *The Business Planning Guide*, by David Bangs.

The students' semester grade was largely dependent upon the team preparation of the business plan, which required each member independently to prepare the ideas for the plan, based upon the facts they had been given. However, the class did not have to use the facts I had given them in establishing a real estate company. If they could agree on an alternative venture, I allowed them select their own subject.

The team was required to meet together and draft a preliminary business plan that was presented to me for criticism, comment and suggestions. Final copies were to be prepared and distributed to each member of the class, with two copies for me. Each of the teams knew that the balance of the class was acting as The Miller Venture Capitalist Company (MVCC). Every team member had to be fully prepared to defend the entire business plan. They would not know in advance when I would interrupt the presentation and ask another to carry on. MVCC was instructed to review the business plan strenuously.

The presentation was limited to 15 minutes, with time to answer questions raised by MVCC, listen to criticism, and answer and defend their position. MVCC would then have a private meeting to discuss the business plan, its presentation, make comments, and finally vote as to whether they would invest their funds in this start-up company. Reasons for their conclusions had to be presented to the entire class, including me. Some of the students dreaded making a presentation to the entire class. Their misgivings were short-lived, however. Each student had the real experience of preparing a business plan, then working with a team for the final business plan, then presenting it to a venture capitalist company. My students loved this program and I hope you will too, because it is a necessity to get you one step closer to the future you desire as a successful entrepreneur.

As my student, you are required to do the following:

1. Study this book.
2. Prepare a business plan for your entrepreneurial business.
3. In preparing your plan, you will quickly discover questions of your own, and you must answer these questions as well.
4. The final business plan will be critiqued by the accounting firm that you have selected. Ask them to hold your "feet to the fire." This will help prepare you for the actual presentation to a venture capitalist firm. The

accounting firm will be acting as venture capitalists and you should ask them whether they would make an investment in your fledgling enterprise. In reviewing your business plan, the accounting firm will be able to ask you questions and learn much more about your potential business, helping you identify ways to trim costs and gather the resources necessary to proceed.

After the business plan has been finalized, it should be presented to your bank for review. Ask for suggestions, criticisms and comments. Ask whether the bank has a venture capitalist fund and ask to meet with these people. All of the above will better prepare you for your meeting with potential venture capitalists and other financial sources.

A business plan should be a roadmap, and it should be a straightforward one. When you approach a source for investments such as venture capitalists, investment bankers, business partners, state and federal sources and others, they will review your business plan in detail, meet with you, question you and then make a decision.

So that you can benefit from the same exercise used with my students, I am enclosing a set of facts for establishing a real estate office, which you can find in the Appendix. These facts were given to my students for the team preparation and presentation. I would strongly urge that you practice preparing a business plan using these real estate facts. It will be a useful exercise and help you create a plan for your own enterprise. In the Appendix you will also find a copy of a business plan prepared by one of my student teams; I thought it was outstanding. After you have completed your plan, compare it with this team's excellent model.

NECESSARY ENTREPRENEURIAL INGREDIENTS

A. ACCOUNTING FIRM

Do not go to a large accounting firm, as you will not yet be considered an important client. A small firm, with perhaps ten to twelve partners, is sufficient. Request someone that has previous experience in preparing a business plan. Ask for permission to contact their clients. The firm should not object. You will be able to evaluate the quality of the work that your accountant has accomplished. You are spending your money and these are the requirements which you must impose. As with all professionals, establish an hourly rate and a budget. The final business plan, prepared by the accounting firm, should be <u>carefully</u> reviewed by you and you <u>must</u> understand every aspect of it. If you have any questions or doubts, meet with the accountants until you are satisfied that you completely understand everything. Failure to do so may leave you in a position of not being able to answer questions posed by venture capitalists or other investors. They will be experienced and skilled interrogators, so you must be as prepared as possible.

B. MARKET RESEARCH

You have determined a demand for your product or service, but your business plan must provide proof that this market demand exists. Investors will not simply take your word for it. I strongly recommend that you hire a qualified market research firm to acquire this proof. I have used Leo Shapiro & Associates, a Chicago-based market research firm, with outstanding results for over twenty-five years. Ask for Leo Shapiro, founder of the company, or George Rosenbaum, president.

Quality market research can do much more than identify market demand for your venture. It can provide you with a number of other insights that can be helpful as you build your business. For example, research can help you determine the proper selling price of your product. If the price is too high, you will not succeed. If the cost of producing the product is more than you can sell it for, you will not succeed either. Market research can also help you identify competition, as well as potential hazards. In my own case, research uncovered a hazard early enough for me to change the direction of the conversion of THE CENTURY, a magnificent building in Manhattan, into condominiums.

Market research typically can't tell you the precise size of your market because only time will reveal your ultimate market share. However, a market research firm like Leo Shapiro & Associates can confirm that you do have a market for your products and the potential to succeed. As always, set a budget in advance. But realize that your quest should not stop with your initial research. Market research should be an ongoing process as you advance into your business. For one thing, it can assist your advertising agency and your public relations firm in optimizing returns from your investment.

DISCUSSION

SANDBURG VILLAGE

The conversion of Sandburg Village, Chicago, which I purchased in 1979 for $105 million, was reported at the time to have been the highest price ever paid for a residential project. The 2,600 units were converted into condominiums in three 30-day selling periods. It was a great achievement. The continued market research enabled me to determine that:

1.   My primary market was the existing tenants in the buildings.

2. The prices I had established were acceptable to the buyers.

3. In my Tuesday morning meetings with my sales staff, market research, advertising and public relations people, a report was distributed to review the sales for the previous week and address problems that had arisen during the week. There was a broad discussion. Input was also received from market research, advertising and public relations. The market research report was always extremely important. George Rosenbaum, of Leo Shapiro & Associates, was able to point out that research had determined one-third of the tenants would buy, one-third were undecided, and one-third would not buy. This enabled me to direct my experienced sales staff to stop calling upon the tenants that would buy, and to instead turn their attention toward the undecided tenants. My sales staff discussed the undecided buyers and we came up with strategies for turning them into buyers. Our efforts were successful. In the first four buildings of Sandburg Village, approximately 70% of the tenants purchased their apartments. The market research, coupled with a continuous advertising campaign and public relations, was critical for this success. All of the advertising and public relations was apparently directed to the general public, but in fact was actually directed to *my* market: the tenants in the building. The major advertising was coupled with discount coupons that allowed a potential buyer to secure a discount and priority to obtain a condominium unit. The coupon program, coupled with a $500 deposit, was a tremendous success. Many of the deposits were returned, and an additional coupon provided, if the buyer desired a priority position on Phase II. This was also very successful. Success can create a snowball effect, as it did in this case; the remaining five buildings sold out quickly.

4. Market research, in addition to determining demand for your product, is an ongoing exercise in risk management. The continued research will enable you to anticipate future hazards, which could make or break you, and you will be able to make timely revisions to your business plan along the way.

C. ADVERTISING

As with an accounting firm, a small advertising agency will give you better service than a large agency because your status as a client will be more important to them. Explain in detail what you have learned from your own market research and give the agency a copy of the research prepared by a qualified firm. Your advertising agency should work closely with your market research people and vice-versa.

Timely meetings should be held, which you must attend. An advertising executive will lead the meetings and question you about your product and what you hope to achieve in reaching your audience. The agency will want to understand your needs before recommending a media campaign to reach your target audience.

The agency should have all of the outside resources that can be brought in. Again, establish your fees in advance. Also, review closely and understand their proposed program that may have to be modified as your marketing efforts continue. In addition, remember that your market research should continue. Your ideas are important and will help them.

D. PUBLIC RELATIONS

Public relations handles all communications with the public that aren't being handled through advertising, such as mentions in metropolitan and community newspapers and magazine articles, on the radio and on TV. Public relations breaks down into two essential components:

1. Having your story brought to the attention of the public, and
2. Crisis Management

BRINGING YOUR STORY TO THE PUBLIC

The entire publishing media, whether printed or electronic, television, newspapers, magazines, the radio, and so on, require materials that will be interesting and important to their audience. The editors of these publications are always seeking interesting and relevant material. A good public relations firm will supply the media with your story on a consistent basis. A published feature or small article has a degree of authenticity and integrity that advertising can't supply. This is the "big bang for the buck" public relations can provide for a retainer or per-cost story charged to you by your PR firm.

CRISIS MANAGEMENT

Another essential is the public relations firm's ability to foresee or eliminate the impact of a pending crisis. The pending problem can't always be seen until it has reached the crisis stage, however, in which case you'll need help for damage control. Since you will be dealing regularly with your PR representatives, keep them up to date on how things are developing. They may recognize a potential crisis that you were unaware of, and advise you on how to manage it.

Your public relations representatives will meet with newspaper editors, or in the case of electronic media, the producers of a program, and be able to reduce the impact of the crisis. In electronic media, such as television, it is the producer that controls the material seen on the screen. The person on the screen is called "the talent." They will have some input, but it is the producer who is the boss.

DISCUSSION

Let me share my own experience when a public relations firm was tremendously helpful:

In Sandburg Village, a serious crisis occurred in the initial stage of conversion. Since Sandburg Village was the largest conversion of apartments in history, it was of extreme importance as a news story. We learned that Bill Kurtis, and his associate Walter Jacobson, were doing a fifteen-minute segment on the conversion of Sandburg Village during CBS local prime-time television. We learned that their story was going to state that I did not actually own the buildings, and that the buildings contained a potential hazard because of falling concrete. I met with my attorneys and my public relations representative, Allen Rafalson. Together we found we had evidence as to the following:

1. Chicago Title and Trust Co. had issued owner's policies showing that I did own the buildings.

2. That the dangerous condition had been fully disclosed to the tenants, and that the remedial construction work to remove these hazards was already in progress.

Rafalson met with the producer of the program earlier in the day. That evening, the 15-minute program had the cameras zoom in on the beautiful flowered malls filled with children playing. The cameras then zoomed in on the construction work in progress. Kurtis explained that the necessary repairs were already in progress.

We had been running full-page ads in the *Chicago Tribune* newspaper. Kurtis took one of the full-page ads and put it on the screen. Of course, the ads showed Sandburg Village at its full potential, completely transformed.

It also showed the discounts that were available on a studio, one-bedroom or two-bedroom apartment. Kurtis then advised the audience that these discounts were available if they sent in the coupon with a deposit of $500 by 8:00pm the forthcoming Saturday. Kurtis was, in effect, selling Sandburg Village for me. Neither he nor Jacobson, nor CBS ever asked for or were ever paid any money. The 15-minute segment, if it had been an advertising spot, would have cost several million dollars.

Rafalson had taken a crisis that could have doomed the project and turned the occasion into an opportunity, which was a magnificent success. His agency was on a monthly retainer. The value of his results, both in obtaining coverage and in crisis management, far exceeded the retainer. That's why public relations can give you such a BIG BANG FOR THE BUCK.

I recommend hiring a small PR firm because you will be a more important client to them. Have the firm prepare a program for you and review it carefully with them. Give them any information as to your market research and have them work closely with your advertising and market research firms. It is necessary to have a team of three—advertising, market research and PR—for best results. I personally worked with Allen Rafalson, president of Rafalson Marketing Communications, Inc. It's a small operation, but by far the best I have ever encountered. Rafalson was able to place ongoing stories on Sandburg Village in the *Chicago Tribune* and *Chicago Sun Times*, which added to the interest of the proposed buyers (the tenants) and the general public. It was a tremendous help.

Allen Rafalson, President
Rafalson Marketing Communications, Inc.
18219 S. Morgan Street, Suite 1S
Homewood, Illinois 60430
312-909-1413
araffles33@yahoo.com

Spend a few minutes reviewing the section on the negotiations, acquisition, financing and conversion of Sandburg Village in 1979-80. The purchase price was $105 million (in today's dollars over $200 million). The project was a phenomenal success. There is much to be learned in this case study.

ASK YOUR BANKER FOR RECOMMENDATIONS

Your bank has many resources, and you should take advantage of them. Among other things, your banker can direct you to professionals, such as accountants and lawyers, to help you develop your business plan. Once your banker understands your needs, feels confident that your proposed business has a strong potential for success, and determines that you are a person of integrity, he or she can, and frequently will, contact other bankers in larger banks to help, and/or recommend potential investors.

E. ATTORNEYS

For starters, ask your bank and accountants for the names of three lawyers who have set up small businesses for beginning entrepreneurs. Do not go to a large law firm, either. Again, in a large firm you will not be considered an important client. Closely question the attorneys' experience in establishing the necessary legal framework for an entrepreneur's business. I would strongly suggest that you set up a small corporation with one class of stock in which you own 100%. The setup costs should be small. As you proceed in your business, the corporation can be expanded with different classes of stock, including non-voting stock. Your experienced lawyers can assist and guide you as you expand. Meet with them but be prepared with your questions, and present the questions in writing. This will clarify your thinking and reduce your costs.

Obtain established rates for the senior and junior partners and the support staff. Examine their computer printouts monthly. I have had the sad experience of reviewing printouts from attorneys hired and have found much waste. I am an attorney with many years of experience, and other attorneys were amazed at what I discovered. If you have discovered serious errors on two consecutive printouts, then you should be careful. Are the mistakes intentional? The attorneys are professionals and you must hold them to professional standards. If you have doubts about the integrity of their billing, you may have doubts about their professional integrity as well.

Do not let your lawyers become your investors or your personal friends. If they should commit an act for which they must be discharged, you may find yourself unwilling to take the necessary steps because you don't want to lose an investor or a friendship. Or, if your spouse develops a friendship with your attorney, she or he may not wish to sever the friendship, thereby clouding your business judgment. Unfortunately, over many years as an entrepreneur, I have made the great mistake of becoming close friends with an attorney I had hired. It ended badly on both business and personal levels.

BBB—BANKS, BANKERS AND BROKERS

As an entrepreneur you will need to have a relationship with a financial institution. Even international corporations need banks. Your local community bank is a great resource. In addition to being a provider of funds, it can assist you in developing your business plan by recommending accountants, lawyers and other professionals who have already developed business plans. Your small community bank has arrangements with larger banks, which are *their* resource. Always keep your personal banker informed as to what you are planning and how you are progressing. In many cases the bank may have as much invested in your enterprise as you have. <u>The bank wants you to succeed.</u> With your success they will also grow. <u>Always</u> maintain a friendly and honest relationship. Banks may not be able to fulfill your growing needs, and when that time comes, they may recommend a larger institution.

Any bank that you go to in the future will contact your previous one for confidential information about your integrity and performance as a customer, so the relationship is an important one. Always try to work with the top executive, preferably the president. He can make decisions without going through the usual bureaucracy. The other high-ranking officers can also make decisions, but won't have as much authority.

Establish that you are a person of integrity. You will present your banker with a request for a loan. They will ask the following questions:

1. What is the purpose of the loan?
2. How will it be repaid?
3. What is the security for the loan?

You will provide the bank with a history of business successes (if you have them) and current financial statements. If the bank suspects a lack of integrity, or doesn't think your business plan is very well thought out, they will not lend you money. Your successes in business are the backup for your integrity. They go together. At least annually, obtain copies of your credit report from all of the credit agencies on your personal files. You may be amazed to discover errors that will reflect on your integrity, and it is essential that these be corrected. Such corrections are not always easy, but persistence makes them possible.

DO NOT PUT ALL OF YOUR EGGS INTO ONE (BANK) BASKET

In borrowing funds from a bank, you will sign a Promissory Note. This is a long, complicated legal document drawn for the *benefit of the lender*. You would have to be an experienced financial lawyer to understand the implications that benefit the lender and limit your powers. The bank will rarely change these provisions unless you are a <u>very</u> important customer.

As an attorney, I have represented banks and been involved in drafting Promissory Notes. These almost always contain a provision that the bank can virtually TAKE OVER any of your assets, even if those assets are not pledged as security for the loan, often without prior notice. The provisions are usually so general that if the bank feels it is in jeopardy, it may take over all of your funds upon demand, and without notifying you that this is going to happen.

These provisions may seem harsh, but they exist in virtually all promissory notes that I have ever read in over fifty years as a lawyer. I have recently, in conjunction with this book, reviewed a promissory note used by one of our largest banks and have selected provisions which may give you some insight into the strictness of the terms and the few, if any, provisions protecting you. (SEE APPENDIX—PROMISSORY NOTE PROVISIONS)

Once the bank has frozen your assets, your only remedy is to hire a lawyer and go to court—a most expensive procedure in which the outcome may not be in your favor. Time is also against you. Therefore, place some of your assets in other financial institutions or in your spouse's name, or in the custody of a trust company. Your funding bank may not be able to reach these assets which will provide some measure of protection should circumstances take you down that unfortunate road.

The promissory note that I have reviewed consists of six pages of legal language. I have not placed a copy of the promissory note in the index because it would be a waste of your time to try to read and understand the provisions. Instead, I have selected a few key provisions, which will make you aware of some of the potential problems that may occur.

The best way to avoid such a calamity is to always keep your banker informed of your business operations, especially if you foresee any potential problems. Bankers understand that there may be problems in every venture. If you work closely with them, they will be much more likely to help you resolve the situation amicably.

However, if bankers are forced to take over a defaulted loan, they will do the following:

1. Set up a reserve for potential losses, reducing a degree of capital that could be used for lending purposes.

2. Have an executive involved in working out the problems. The bank would rather recast the loan and its provisions in order to avoid a failure.

3. In housing, an empty house causes a serious deterioration of the dwelling. Even if the house is leased, the lessee will not keep it in good condition, which you as an owner would do. Also, in the business world, the business could deteriorate because you are no longer personally involved.

DISCUSSION

RESERVE SAVINGS AND LOAN ASSOCIATION, ELMHURST, IL
In the 1960's, with a partner (a banker), we acquired the ownership of the stock of Reserve Savings & Loan Association located in Elmhurst, IL. I had established a close working relationship with the Michigan Avenue National Bank of Chicago and the president loaned us the necessary funds towards acquisition. I had been working closely with an executive vice president and he was fully informed as to

my years of successful business dealings, my condo conversions and future plans. I frequently met with him and informed him of my activities. My credit file was firmly established. My information was passed on to the president. I established a relationship with him and informed him of my plans for purchasing and improving Reserve Savings & Loan Association. He approved the requested loan. I kept the president fully informed of my activities at Reserve Savings, and of all other business activities on a timely basis.

As part of the deal, I ended up becoming the president of Reserve Savings & Loan, and found myself in the unique position of being on the lending side of the desk. This was a great learning experience. My partner was a silent partner and was not involved. He preferred to spend all of his time as head of his small bank.

Reserve Savings was an old institution, originally located on the west side of Chicago, which had moved to Elmhurst a few years earlier. Stock savings and loan associations were no longer chartered in Illinois. Reserve Savings was grandfathered as a stock institution. I discovered that Reserve Savings was virtually unknown in the community. I undertook to market Reserve Savings to the community. Local institutions, such as the Kiwanis Club, were invited to use the meeting rooms on the lower level in the evenings. We provided coffee and sweets. Through such outreach efforts, the name Reserve Savings quickly spread through the community.

Here's another example of how I helped spread Reserve Savings' name through the community: The local high school football team was playing for the championship. I hired a radio station to broadcast the game and I arranged to have Reserve Savings frequently mentioned. The game was heard by the entire community. The assets of Reserve Savings virtually doubled in three years and the profits greatly increased. Ultimately, a group of investors purchased my interest in the bank, and my partner sold a portion of his interest. I returned to my highly profitable business of converting apartment buildings. Michigan Avenue National Bank was fully repaid both in principal and interest, according to the requirements of the loan agreement.

MID-CITY NATIONAL BANK OF CHICAGO was owned by a family of bankers with roots going back several hundred years. They had a policy of promoting their officers. In the early 1940's, I was dealing with this well-established institution. I met with the president, presented to him my need for a loan, and outlined how I would repay the loan. He listened, and then proceeded to explain the errors in my thinking. I left disappointed. Upon later reflection, I determined that he was correct and I should have been thankful for his insight and advice.

Because of their broader experience, a banker can sometimes determine potential hazards to your business that you did not anticipate, and may refuse to approve the loan. But they should do so with an explanation, and if nothing else, this exchange will benefit you and improve your relationship with the banker. Remember, this might not be your only discussion; it may simply be a prelude to a meeting with a more favorable outcome.

CONTINENTAL ILLINOIS BANK AND TRUST COMPANY was the fourth or fifth largest bank in the U.S. I recognized that Michigan National Bank, a small national bank, did not have the necessary lending power needed and discussed this with the president. He fully understood, agreed that I was going to need to work with a larger bank and recommended Continental Bank. However, I still maintained a small account with Michigan National.

At Continental Bank, I was introduced to Reinhardt Schneider, a lending officer, and worked closely with him. I established a credit file and, wherever possible, attempted to make my account very profitable for the bank.

In the mid-1950's, I acquired an apartment building at 5401 S. Hyde Park Blvd., in Chicago. This building was an excellent candidate for conversion to condominiums. I was able to obtain an option for the purchase, but with the right to convert the building during the term of the option. I guaranteed any rental loss.

A loan was arranged with Mr. Schneider in the event funds should become necessary. To open this loan would cost me $80,000. Through my many years as a real estate lawyer, I understood that the use of Chicago Title and Trust Company escrows could provide a method of acquiring the building without resorting to a loan. After the sufficient sales had been made, the buyers and their lenders would deposit their funds into separate escrows with Chicago Title and Trust Co. The owner of 5401 S. Hyde Park would deposit his deed of conveyance into a separate escrow. After Chicago Title examined the title and issued its own title and mortgage insurance policies, Chicago Title would transfer the buyer's funds into the seller's escrow account. At that point, the seller's deed of conveyance was recorded. The seller received his funds and the various buyers received the title policies. The remaining unsold units remained my property for future sales.

There were sufficient funds to pay the seller, therefore I did not need Continental Bank's loan. The question I had to ask myself was: Should I or shouldn't I open the bank loan? I did not need the loan, and I could have saved $80,000. However, I wanted to improve my credit file. So, I called Reinhardt and arranged to have him meet with me at Chicago Title on a Friday afternoon and, while sitting there, I repaid half of his loan. The following Wednesday, the entire loan was repaid. He called to tell me that the $80,000 I paid earned significant interest for the bank in just a few days, and that this demonstrated that his department had been very profitable during that month. All of this improved my credit file.

Doug Hall, a high-ranking executive of the bank, met with me and gave me the greatest compliment I had ever expected to receive. "Harold, the bank is going to lend you the $105 million needed for the purchase of Sandburg Village. However, the bank will not loan you more because you are reaching the lending limit of this bank and <u>YOU ARE NOT STANDARD OIL OF INDIANA</u>." My wife and I started our marriage with $1,200 in wedding gifts. To have placed me in the same sentence as Standard Oil of Indiana was the greatest business compliment I have ever received! I had, over many years, acquired a reputation of integrity, business success and hard work.

BUSINESS HAZARDS: A PERSONAL EXPERIENCE

WILLOUGBY, CHEVY CHASE, MARYLAND

I promoted my CFO to the position of president of First Condominium Development Co. He had the authority to acquire apartment buildings. He purchased the Willoughby in Chevy Chase, Maryland, a property that had all of the requirements for a successful conversion. I learned that the man I had promoted to president of the company had entered into a secret partnership with my lawyer. They were stealing deals from my company. The president was immediately fired and my relationship with the law firm terminated. My wife and I moved into the Willoughby and I undertook to complete the conversion. I have always had a "hands on" policy in the conversion of apartment buildings.

During the Carter administration, mortgage interest rates rose to between 17% and 18%. Because of these historically high interest rates, even qualified buyers would not proceed. This I understood. I knew that it would only be a period of time before interest rates would plunge back down to 7 to 8%. The holding period, however, would be expensive. To protect yourself against extremely high interest rates, arrange to purchase from the bank mortgage funds with an interest rate ceiling and floor. The banks will do this for a fee. With the Sandburg Village condo conversion, during Phase 3, I had detected that interest rates would again be above the normal range. I arranged with the CFO to have the necessary funds, which were in the millions, for a set fee of $800,000. This gave me the insurance that my buyers could close. Because of my knowledge of financial markets, I was able to save the $800,000 by determining in advance where the mortgage interest rates would be for a period of six months.

The Continental Illinois Bank had many loans to other condo converters. The bank felt that these loans were in jeopardy because of the high interest rates and sent its officers to the various condo conversions throughout the country to review their status. I met with the officers and took them into a model apartment. It was lunchtime. My wife heard me talking with the officers at the model apartment and came out wearing her apron. I explained to the officers that we had moved into the Willoughby to personally guide it through this difficult period. The bank officers reported our decision back to their superiors. Eventually, when interest rates came back down to normal, the approximately 70% of tenants who had purchased their apartments closed and the balance of the building was sold out. As a condo conversion it was successful, but it was a financial disaster because the holding action caused a great loss in interest and other expenses. The Continental Bank subsequently reduced its lending to most condo converters. I, however, was invited to continue.

Not only had I worked hard to establish an excellent reputation and history with the bank, I was willing to assume personal responsibility to guide the Willoughby project to success. This is just one example of why establishing your personal integrity is extremely important to an entrepreneur.

In dealing with a bank, you are dealing with the individual bankers. In going to a new bank, <u>always</u> find a personal banker that has experience in your area of business. Otherwise, you are starting at ground zero in teaching them about your business field. The banker will want to know the purpose of the loan, how it will be repaid, and the security for the loan. Above all, the bank will investigate, through its various resources, your previous experiences and integrity as a businessperson. If, however, the bank feels you do not have integrity, they will not lend you a dime.

Always keep your banker fully informed as to what you are seeking to accomplish. If he is convinced that the loan you are requesting is a "safe" loan, he will try to sell it to the loan committee. In effect, he becomes your salesman. If he leaves the bank and goes to another bank, go with him. You have already established an important relationship, and this will carry over to the new institution.

Bankers always want to be informed as to your successes, but, as I stated before, always keep them informed of potential problems as well. They don't want to be suddenly confronted with a bad loan. They will work with you to reform and possibly reconstruct the loan by postponing or reducing interest and principal payments and so on. However, they will only do so if you have worked with them from the inception of the loan and have been honest about warning them of potential problems. If a loan goes into default, the bank is required by law to do the following:

1. Set up a reserve for potential losses.

2. Assign an officer to supervise the defaulted loan.

3. The defaulting loan will usually deteriorate in its value.

4. A lawsuit may be filed, creating an additional problem for the bank. Therefore, the bank will usually work with you to prevent a default.

LESSONS TO BE LEARNED

1. Work with a banker that already knows your industry.

2. Keep your bankers fully informed as to the progress of your venture, both the pluses and potential problems. They understand that all loans may have potential problems.

3. Ask your banker for advice. He will give it to you freely, because he wants you to succeed.

4. Do not go to another banking institution without consulting your current bank, because your existing bank will probably learn of this and be unhappy. Resort to this only when your new financial institution is an important improvement over your existing one. For example, I informed the president of Michigan Avenue National Bank that I was going to the Continental Illinois Bank, and he fully understood my reasons. We remained good friends.

5. It is important to lock in mortgage loans for purchases with interest rates that have a ceiling and a floor in advance of your project. Banks will consider doing this because they can always hedge their loans. The cost is worth incurring; it is like buying an insurance policy.

6. The Continental Bank requested that I continue to borrow from them. Unfortunately, many other developers were locked out, but I had established a favorable reputation and history with this major banking institution, which turned out to be quite valuable.

YOUR CREDIT FILE

A well-established credit file is essential. The credit file is a complete history of your business dealings, credit reports and all other essential information, including your transactions with the bank.

In the mid 1950's, I read a feature article by Jesse Jones (not Jesse James!), a small-town businessman in Texas who realized that without credit, you are like a "dead man." He started borrowing small sums of money from his local bank, which he always re-paid on time or even early. Many times he did not have any real need for the funds. By doing this, he built up a "<u>credit file</u>." An opportunity arose in which he needed a loan that was much larger than any loan he had previously obtained. Based upon his credit file, the loan was granted. Mr. Jones went on to become an extremely successful businessman and multi-millionaire.

During the Great Depression, President Franklin Delano Roosevelt, with the assistance of a Democratic Congress, introduced a series of programs so that the country could emerge from the depths of the Great Depression. This is part of my life story. Today, when we encounter five-, six-or seven-percent unemployment, we consider this to be quite a problem. However, during the Great Depression, unemployment was 25% or more. Neighborhood businesses, grocery stores and many shops were closed. People were sleeping on park benches. There were bread lines. State Street, Chicago's most important commercial street, was closed. All of the major retail stores were dark.

As a kid, I was always a good saver and would deposit my nickels, dimes and quarters in my local bank. One day, I was on the bank floor waiting in a long line to withdraw my fortune, eight to ten dollars. In those days, the teller windows had horizontal golden bars that could be raised or lowered. There was a large crowd outside. Suddenly, all of the tellers closed their windows. THE BANK WAS OUT OF BUSINESS! The people were screaming and crying. They were wiped out.

I can remember this terrible episode as if it were yesterday. Insurance on bank deposits did not come into existence until Franklin Delano Roosevelt and a Democratic Congress instituted deposit insurance on all bank accounts.

In dictating this paragraph, I'm recalling as if it was this morning when that dreadful episode took place. Seventy-five years later, it still hurts. I was too young to comprehend fully what had taken place, but the event changed my life. As an entrepreneur, I always took measured risk but I was never a gambler. President Roosevelt declared a "bank holiday." All of the banks in the United States were temporarily closed to reorganize. Gradually, the country grew out of the dreadful Great Depression. The Roosevelt administration also introduced many other programs, including the Work Progress Administration, which put architects and builders to work to construct post offices throughout the United States. Artists were hired to create beautiful murals. Unemployed teenagers and young men were given the opportunity to go to construction camps, where they were fed, lived in dormitories and paid. These men helped reforest the country.

Jesse Jones was placed in charge of the Reconstruction Finance Corporation. His responsibility was to inject federal funds into businesses and industries to help jump-start and invigorate the economy. It worked.

The Great Depression and lessons I had learned from Jones made me determined to build up a credit file. I gave the banks every opportunity to earn money through my relationship with them, even sometimes at my own expense. It was a worthwhile investment.

BROKERS

Business brokers are another source of funds for an entrepreneur. A broker rarely lends his or her own funds. They broker your requests with a source of funds.

They may charge you an up-front fee. Pay only a small start-up fee. Establish your costs, how much money they will raise for you, and other essential details. Your accountants can help you. Check out these brokers with your banker before paying them, however. There are reliable brokers, but there are also unreliable ones—so always ask the broker for the names and phone numbers of previously satisfied customers.

VENTURE CAPITALISTS

Large banks may have a venture capital division. Your local bank may be able to direct you to a bank with a venture-capital division. Federal and state sponsored investment funds are also available, but the process is an arduous one and the funds can take a long time to materialize. There are many private venture capital funds as well, all with specific specializations, interests and requirements. Your bank, accountant and lawyer may be able to direct you towards a venture capital firm that you can work with. If your business venture aligns with their mission and goals, a deal may eventually be struck—but if not, they aren't likely to invest in your company.

In any case, developing a working relationship with venture capitalists is a complex process that will require the help of both an accountant and lawyer. It's also a step in the building of a business that can't be taken lightly. Venture capital can help grow a business faster than it might otherwise, but the money comes with strings attached. Venture capitalists will probably want an ownership stake in the business, and will hold you accountable for the business's performance. They may also charge other fees against the money they lend you. Whatever you do, make certain that you research the history of the fund, the type of investment the funders are seeking, and the amount they are willing to invest, along with the lending terms. And remember, even if you are successful in gaining the support of venture capitalists, be aware that in taking venture capital money, you are also giving up some control of your business. *The key is to always retain sufficient stock in your company to maintain control.* Otherwise, you could lose your own company.

Nevertheless, a venture capitalist can be of benefit in the following areas:

1. A critical analysis of your business plan.
2. Concluding, to their satisfaction, whether you are capable of carrying on your enterprise.
3. Providing the necessary funds.

4. Suggesting that you hire professional management, since, as an entrepreneur, you may not have the training, experience or knowledge for a larger business.

5. Assisting you to determine if your company should go public.

6. Acquiring or merging with other companies.

If you are successful in your start-up business, you may be able to generate sufficient funds for growth on your own—and that is the preferable way to go. Venture capital is sometimes necessary, but the longer you can do without it, the better.

STOCKBROKERS

Stockbrokers earn their income on commission fees generated by their customers buying or selling stocks, bonds and other such securities. Do not consider stockbrokers independent financial advisors. They have a conflict of interest. In most stock brokerage firms, the licensed stockbroker will be given a list each morning as to the investments they should push. Be cautious. Many reliable large brokerage firms strongly advised their clients to invest in Enron, WorldCom, and Global Crossing, which collectively suffered some of the worst corporate bankruptcies in U.S. history. All of these companies proved disastrous for the investors. Many of these brokerage firms were sued by their customers as a result.

FINANCIAL ADVISORS

An experienced, seasoned financial advisor will be a most reliable and valuable source of information. Financial advisors are paid an agreed-upon fee. They will not be involved in a conflict of interest, since their earnings are not based upon your buying or selling investments. I have used financial advisors with great success. A bank can also provide valuable financial advice.

REAL ESTATE BROKERS

Real estate brokers are not your financial advisors. They earn their income through commission, based on a percentage of the selling price, paid by the seller (and sometimes by the buyer). Since their income is based upon your buying or selling, you must be cautious about the advice they give to you. Ask your real estate broker for a list of three other comparable pieces of real estate that have been sold in the last three months. Study these printouts. Also, ask your broker for a copy of the listing sheets, which will give you much more detail than the printouts. A real estate broker also has a source for mortgage funds. Check out their sources against the information available online.

Always, *always* be represented by an experienced real estate lawyer. Purchasing or selling properties requires going through an involved legal process. Your lawyer can save you a great deal of money, time and worry. Proceeding without a lawyer is a hazard.

STRUCTURING YOUR BUSINESS

PARTNERSHIPS

You may form small partnerships while you are raising initial capital. This is usually a necessary approach. A partnership has advantages but has one serious hazard: any partner who has the authority as a partner may undertake an action that may damage or destroy the partnership. Forming a small corporation can prevent this. This is discussed more fully in the YOUR BUSINESS PLAN section under ATTORNEYS.

Your partners or investors should invest cash. Their time has value but once the investment is lost, the lost time is forgotten. However, when cash is involved, they will work diligently to try to recover their investment, which better ensures that your business will succeed.

LIMITED PARTNERSHIPS

This is a business vehicle, or formation, created by statute. The investors' liability is limited to their investment. They are also restricted from having any input into the operation of the limited partnership. The general partner has virtually all of the power and control. If limited partners become involved in the operation, they could claim, in the event litigation becomes necessary, that they had become general partners. The general partner has fiduciary responsibility to keep the limited partners informed, by semi-annual or annual meetings, during which financial information should be disclosed.

A major hazard in a limited partnership is that it is difficult for a limited partner to sell their interest, because there is a limited market and the value is frequently discounted. Also, the amount of interest a limited partner has in the business is a minority interest.

PROPRIETORSHIP

You may start off as a sole proprietor. The great advantage to sole proprietorship is that you are the owner. The disadvantage lies in bringing in additional capital without forming a corporation or partnership. In addition, you must ask yourself who will succeed you and take over your business in the future? A great deal of thought should be given to this. I have seen successful proprietorships turned over to a son or daughter. This is very common. Carefully consider your offspring and select the child that has the talent, experience and motivation to carry on your business. Also consider your spouse.

INFORM YOUR PARTNERS, SHAREHOLDERS, FINANCIAL ADVISORS AND ALL OTHER INTERESTED PARTIES, ON A TIMELY BASIS, OF YOUR ACTIVITIES. NO ONE LIKES SURPRISES, ESPECIALLY WHEN THEY MAY BE NEGATIVE.

Everyone will understand that in all businesses, unforeseen problems may arise. Always act with INTEGRITY. You will head off some of the problems now being encountered by the president and CFO of Enron, a huge corporation that went bankrupt with the loss of billions of dollars to its bankers and shareholders. Both of these officers at Enron are being tried on criminal charges that they failed to disclose the actual financial condition of the corporation and didn't tell the truth to the investors, shareholders and employees. The officers of other large corporations have also been sent to jail for the same reasons.

CORPORATIONS

I would strongly suggest that you set up a small corporation with one class of stock in which you own 100%. The setup costs should be small. As you proceed in your business, the corporation can be expanded with different classes of stock, including non-voting stock. Experienced lawyers can assist and guide you as you expand.

THE MANY HAZARDS

Always be careful and cautious in your business dealings. Here are a few principles that you should follow:

1. Delegate—but always supervise. I personally have made the mistake of delegating authority to an executive, but failing to supervise because I

had become too busy. As described in the Willoughby discussion earlier, this particular individual was unscrupulous and took advantage of the situation.

2. A second signature for control of the issuance of a check can be useful but also useless. The second signature should be delegated to a responsible person completely independent from the first signatory, with the explicit understanding that he should question why the check is being issued. Example: I had a secretary as a second signatory. While she understood her responsibility, she was a weak person. The primary signature was that of an officer of my company who had helped my secretary's son establish a business. Because of that assistance, my secretary became obligated to the primary signatory. Always, on a regular basis, have a third officer not involved with the other two double-check the signatures and the purpose of the check.

3. Banks are now cutting their costs by not returning the original checks, or they will send you a copy of the front of the check. Always require that you receive a copy of the backside of the check, which reveals the endorsement. You will therefore be able to ensure that the check was paid to the proper person.

4. An executive who has misled should be removed. Otherwise, the deceit will continue, and if the lie is discovered but merely dismissed, the consequences will continue. Example: My wife discovered that an executive had issued a check in the amount of $8,000 to settle a dispute and later denied that the matter had been settled. My wife should have had him discharged immediately. Subsequent consequences were costly.

5. Bribery. Once an individual has accepted a bribe, he or she cannot tell the briber that enough is enough. The bribed person cannot go and report the bribery. He or she has already committed a crime. Example: My in-laws had a very famous steak house, which was closed after their death. It was a restaurant where steaks were aged in a special refrigerator. I helped liquidate the business and discovered that many of the packages were mis-labeled. The packages were listed as weighing ten pounds, but in actuality weighed only five pounds. The employee in charge of checking out the purchases took a $50 bribe to allow this deceptive practice, and cost my in-laws thousands of dollars. You cannot protect yourself against bribery. This was in a small business, but bribery can be committed in many ways: doing favors, providing vacations, and so on. Opportunities for bribery are nearly unlimited. Our own government is rife with examples

of bribery. Lobbyists provide legislators with free fancy vacations, free airfare, free expensive dinners, personal favors and so on. President Harry Truman discovered that his Chief of Staff had taken, as a gift, a fur coat for his wife; the man was immediately fired.

6. Extramarital affairs are a common and difficult problem in almost all offices. Sexual attraction is difficult to control, even if the parties are married. Affairs can create a difficult and dangerous situation in your office. Other employees will inevitably become aware of the affair. What to do? In a larger company, if possible, transfer the executive to a different city. If the person will not go, then find grounds for dismissal.

7. Capital: It's difficult to acquire and easy to waste. Your capital should be carefully guarded. Don't let your ego be involved in building large, sumptuous offices or buying unnecessary equipment. Example: An acquaintance of the president of a small savings bank had large, expensive, unnecessarily luxurious headquarters. The capital reserves were dissipated. He asked for my assistance in selling the building. I informed him that no buyer would purchase this large and essentially useless type of building. He was forced out.

8. Guarantor: A fool with a pen. You will frequently be asked to guarantee a loan or a lease. Below are the ways to limit your liability.

    A. Guarantee only the top 10% or 15% of the loan. Frequently, the borrower will have repaid a good portion of this amount.

    B. Agree to only a fixed dollar amount liability. The lender usually wants to make the loan and this limitation will be acceptable.

    C. Leases: they contain many paragraphs, all for the benefit of the lessor. If you guarantee the entire lease, you are opening yourself to many problems. Limit your liability to the payment of the rent.

EXECUTIVES: IMPROVING YOUR PERFORMANCE

PROBLEM SOLVING: A DIFFICULT AND COMMON OCCURRENCE

Abraham Lincoln is an example of a leader who had many problems of the gravest importance, and he developed a method of analyzing and simplifying problems in order to arrive at a solution.

I have been using Abraham Lincoln's method for over 45 years for many problems, both business and personal. The method has been most helpful.

Paper is cheap. I take a pad of paper and head it:

ABRAHAM LINCOLN METHOD

    I.   WHERE AM I NOW? (Page one)

    II. WHAT DO I WANT TO ACCOMPLISH? (Page two)

    III TOOLS FOR ACHIEVING GOALS (Page three)

    VI. CONSEQUENCES IF I FAIL (Page four)

Use separate pages and use this method four or five times. You will discover that it is a most helpful and useful method of solving problems.

ANDREW CARNEGIE

Andrew Carnegie came to the United States as a poor man and became the world's richest man. U.S. Steel was one of his enterprises. Around the year 1900, at a party, a brash young man told Carnegie, "I have a method that can improve your performance." Carnegie told him, "Be at my office at 10:00 a.m. tomorrow morning, and if you can provide a useful method to improve my performance, I will pay you $10,000." (Today it would be $100,000).

The next day the young man asked: at the end of the day, do you frequently discover that there are important calls or items that you have failed to complete? If so, do the following:

1.   Every morning, in random order, make a list of everything that has to be accomplished.

2.   With a red pencil, review and prioritize these items.

3.   If you discover that there is an item that should be inserted, place it between a number that has already been prioritized. List the prior item with a capital A, and the insert with a capital B.

4.   At the end of the day, you will have accomplished and completed the most important tasks.

I check off the completed items on the left margin. To denote the uncompleted items, I place a circle in the right-hand margin.

The following day, AGAIN AT RANDOM, list everything that you have to accomplish and insert the circled items leftover from the prior page. Review this list again with a red pencil and, in the left-hand margin, prioritize the items that have to be accomplished.

Carnegie gave the young man a check for $10,000.

PERSONAL MEMORANDUMS

Relying purely upon your memory can be a fault. You may have forgotten important items, so you should always retain some notes in your personal files. I carry with me a simple electronic device onto which I dictate ideas, memos, and other pertinent information that I can read back quickly. The recording also contains items for my secretary to pursue. You may not be in a position to make a written memo, but this palm-sized device can be carried with you. I recently purchased an Olympus Digital Voice Recorder, available at stationery stores for about $50. It is a most useful and handy device.

Certain memorandums are confidential and you may not want them disclosed to your private secretary. I have seen situations where a secretary leaves the executive and sometimes takes memos that could be very damaging. Carefully screen your memos and keep those that are potentially misinterpreted or damaging away from your secretary or assistant. Keep these in a locked drawer with only one key, which you maintain yourself.

RETURNING PHONE CALLS

Failure to return phone calls is insulting to the caller and can result in a missed opportunity. This has happened to me. I once received a phone call from a competitor, who had asked to purchase a piece of commercial real estate that my father owned. I did not return the call, as I did not believe the caller had the financial capital to make the purchase. This was a serious mistake. I later learned that he had a different approach to acquiring this real estate. Had I dealt with him directly, I would not have offended him, and I would have had better results. Always have your secretary call and explain why you cannot return the call right away, and ask for times that are convenient to return the call.

Keep in mind that a capable secretary is a great asset. He or she can also be a "gatekeeper," and can assure that you are only scheduled for important appointments, and help you keep up with your busy schedule.

HOLIDAY CARDS

A holiday card has no real value in and of itself. During the holiday season, people receive many such cards. Adding your own personal note will give it real value. Have all of your officers, in their own handwriting, insert a personal note.

BOARD OF DIRECTORS: SHOULD I JOIN OR SHOULD I NOT

You may be asked to become a member of a Board of Directors. Your ego may say yes. Your decision should be examined carefully. Being a member of a board can bring you into excellent business contacts and provide you with an exchange of information that could be beneficial. But, board membership has some serious hazards. For instance, there will be important matters that come before the board that you are <u>against</u>. If you are sufficiently against the matter and vote NO, but the decision doesn't go your way, you could be held liable anyway. At some subsequent date, if there is a lawsuit against the corporation, the entire board of Directors can become defendants. Protect yourself. Have the secretary give you a copy of the minutes, which must outline your strong reasons for voting against the issue and your NO vote. Be sure this becomes part of the record of the Board of Directors, and be sure to keep a copy for yourself. If you are named as a defendant, this information may fully protect you. Sit down with the attorneys and prove to them that you should not be a part of this litigation.

The corporation will also be purchasing Directors Liability insurance. This is important for your protection. As with all insurance, it must be properly written with an old-line insurance company. Also, the limits should be large enough to cover unforeseen contingencies.

HOW WE LOST THE WAR TO JAPAN (AUTOS)

Toyota is now larger than Ford. The automobile industry was an American industry and we lost our leadership because of poor quality. The marketing people took over and were of the strong belief that the American public would continue to accept inferior automobiles. Toyota became larger than Ford because of quality of product. Which is more important? You now have the answer.

My brother-in-law had dry cleaning shops in Flint, Michigan where many General Motors autos were being manufactured. He became friendly with men that worked on the production line. I discussed the poor quality of American automobiles and he told me about one of his customers who installed transmissions. When he discovered a defective transmission, he was ordered by his supervisor to place the defective transmission into a huge bin to be returned to the manufacturer.

During the course of the day, in order to continue the production line, the defective transmissions were installed into the automobiles. The supervisor said, "Let the dealers handle this problem."

I always purchased General Motor's Buick LeSabres. Several years ago, I purchased a new Buick LeSabre from a dealer in Evanston, Illinois. When I returned home, my wife told me that when driving back from O'Hare Airport, she noticed there was something wrong with the transmission. She brought the auto back into the dealership and told the service manager that the car should be road tested. He said this would be done.

A day or two later, my wife returned for her car and asked if it had been road tested. The servicer said yes. My wife asked to talk to the mechanic and he said that the car had not been road tested and it should be done while she was still waiting. He returned approximately one hour later and told my wife that she could have been killed in the car because of the transmission.

That was the last American car I ever purchased. I switched to Toyotas and Hondas.

LESSONS FROM THREE GIANTS OF INDUSTRY

ABRAHAM N. PRITZKER

Abraham N. Pritzker (A.N.), the founder of the Pritzker empire; Charles Allen (The Midas of Wall Street); and Arthur Rubloff ("The Man Who Changed the Face of Chicago"), all became my partners and friends, and I learned a great deal from them.

Abraham N. Pritzker, together with his brother, Jack, formed the law firm of Pritzker & Pritzker in Chicago. Their law practice was limited. They were primarily engaged in the world of business. Under the leadership of A.N., the Pritzker empire was created. It is a privately held entity.

A.N. was taken out of high school, enrolled in Harvard and became a Harvard-educated lawyer. He was by far the most outstanding man that I have met in my long lifetime. He became my partner in the conversion of Sandburg Village, and through this relationship became my close friend and mentor. His main interest was negotiating deals. His brother, Jack, worked closely with A.N., but his primary function was real estate deals.

It is estimated that the Pritzker empire has assets between $16 to $17 billion and may control businesses of between $90 to $100 billion. There is no public information; however, as I have been involved with the Pritzker's for over thirty years, the information I have gathered is assumed to be accurate. I dealt almost exclusively with my friend, A.N.

For many years, all investments were acquired and privately held. A.N. told me he did not want any companies with outside shareholders and would frequently buy out shareholders, even paying a premium in order to gain the stock. Over time, the ability to control the investment was worth more than the premium he paid. Keeping his investments privately held ensured that the companies were not subject to examination by the Security and Exchange Commission.

A.N., in a very quiet way, was very charitable. He gave many millions to Michael Reese Hospital, because his father, as a child, the son of poor Jewish immigrants from Russia, was hospitalized and did not own a coat. The nurses at Michael Reese bought him a coat so he could be released from the hospital during a bitter Chicago winter. A.N. emotionally told me, "How can I ever repay Michael Reese for what they did for my father?" He gave many millions to rescue the Jews from Ethiopia, and millions more to educational and charitable institutions.

A.N. died in his early nineties. His mind was active and he was physically able to carry on, even at an advanced age. I knew him well and we spent many, many hours together. He never smoked, drank or gambled. He lived a very moderate life.

LESSONS LEARNED FROM A.N.

1. In every partnership, the partner was required to invest cash. A partner will work diligently to assist in recovering his cash investment. Time, once lost, is written off.

2. Acquisitions of large corporations are difficult. It is better to acquire two or three smaller corporations, which in totality will add up to the large corporation. Negotiations are always done on a private and friendly basis.

3. Always protect your money sources. The Pritzkers have had a relationship with the Prudential Insurance Co., probably dating back eighty years. Many of the Hyatt Hotels are owned jointly or managed by the Pritzker's for Prudential.

4. First National Bank of Chicago has also been a primary source of funds for the Pritzkers for perhaps over eighty years. The relationship was such that a phone call to the CEO of First National explaining the reason for the loan and other details was usually all that was necessary. The required paperwork followed.

5. When negotiating a purchase deal, being able to tell the seller that you do not need to acquire funding can facilitate the deal.

6. A.N. and his brother Jack had the authority to make decisions, as did A.N.'s sons, Jay, Robert and Donald. They consulted with one another. However, the laborious and time-consuming requirement of a Board of Director's approval was not required, as this was a privately held entity.

7. The money sources were always protected, and, in the event of a failed bank loan, the Pritzker's would work diligently so the bank would not suffer any loss.

8. Integrity was the cornerstone of the Pritzkers in all of their business dealings.

9. A.N. quietly gave great sums of monies to various charities.

10. Valued and trustworthy employees were richly rewarded.

CHARLES ALLEN

Charles Allen, "The Midas of Wall Street," became my partner in approximately 1983, when I purchased The Century, an outstanding apartment building on the west side of Central Park, Manhattan, for conversion. I asked my partner and friend, Arthur Rubloff, to join me, and he suggested that I invite Allen to also become a partner. Charles and his brother, Herb, had been partners with Arthur for over forty years in many business ventures and the Allens were Arthur's financial source.

Charlie was born in 1903 to an impoverished family with five children. He never finished high school. At age fifteen, he became a runner on the New York Stock Exchange and his brother Herb joined him shortly thereafter. Stock quotations were written on huge blackboards with changes updated in chalk. This was long before the age of electronics!

Charlie devoted his entire life to studying and investing in the stock market. His nephew, Herb Jr., told me that every day he obtained the early copy of the *Wall Street Journal*, which he studied. Both Charlie and Herb were experts on dealings in the stock exchange. The stock exchange is a misnomer: it is really a MARKET OF STOCKS. The brothers were successful and, in 1929, sensing a vastly overpriced, inflated stock market, Herb convinced Charlie to sell the stock market <u>SHORT</u>. The 1929 Stock Market crash enabled the brothers to have millions of dollars in CASH. The buying power of one million dollars during The Great Depression was probably equal to at least one hundred million dollars today.

They were thus able to buy large blocks of stock in viable corporations at bargain prices. They bought the magnificent Plaza Hotel, in Manhattan, for $7 million.

In approximately 1930, a great collector of Picasso, Toulouse-Lautrec, Gauguin, and other great painters, was in need of cash. Banks are always reluctant to lend money on art since the exact value is unknown. Charles always had an interest in art and loaned the collector $50,000, an amount secured by this vast art collection. The loan was to be redeemed within six months. It was never redeemed.

In approximately 1982, with Charles' permission, Arthur took me through Charles' apartment at the Sherry Neverlands and, hanging on the walls, were original Picasso's, Gaugiun's Toulouse-Lautrec's, a small portion of the vast collection still held in the bank vaults. I would estimate that the collection had a value of several billion dollars. Cash is not King. CASH IS POWER.

Charlie was a very quiet, unassuming man. He used taxicabs while many of his family members were chauffeured throughout Manhattan. The family donated $15 million to Columbia Presbyterian Medical Center in memory of their mother, Frances.

Major investments were also made in the Syntex Corporation, the Teleregister Corp., and oil fields in many parts of the world. In addition, Charles was a member of the Board of Directors of Pepsi Cola and other major corporations.

The Irvine Ranch in Orange County, CA., owned by descendents of the original family, became involved in a family dispute. A group of wealthy investors including the Allens, Arthur Rubloff and others, formed a syndicate to purchase the Irvine Ranch. One of the members of the family involved in the dispute was also one of the partners. The Irvine Ranch became the largest master-planned urban development in the U.S. Today, Disneyland is located in the former Irvine Ranch.

LESSONS TO BE LEARNED

1. Charlie and Herb became experts in their knowledge of the stock market and this continued for a lifetime.

2. Because of this knowledge, they sensed that, in 1929, the stock market was grossly overpriced and there would be a major crash.

3. In selling the market SHORT, they accumulated great sums of cash.

4. Cash is more important than being King; CASH IS POWER.

5. Cash was in extremely short supply due to the Great Depression, which lasted for approximately ten years.

6. Their cash enabled them to buy vast holdings of secure and important corporations at bargain basement prices.

7.   The brothers were thrifty and extremely hard working.

8.   The Allens had found an area in the stock market that remained their focus for a lifetime. Their lifelong interest in the stock market gave them the zeal to continue participating in the market of stocks. Charles died at age 91 in 1994.

ARTHUR RUBLOFF

Arthur Rubloff became my partner in approximately 1977, when Arthur and the Allens entered into a sales contract, whereby I purchased UNIVERSITY PARK, an outstanding rental apartment building of approximately 540 rental units, located in the vicinity of the University of Chicago. The agreement provided that if the net profits exceeded a certain amount, the additional profits would be split 50/50. I was responsible for all of the costs of conversion, rehab, advertising, upgrading and many other items, totaling several hundred thousand dollars. It was a financial success and the profits exceeded the original selling price. Arthur and the Allens received a much greater price for the property than they had anticipated.

Arthur had an international reputation in real estate, and his career spanned approximately sixty years. He developed Evergreen Shopping Plaza in Chicago, one of the earliest shopping centers in the U.S. The Magnificent Mile, which he helped develop and named, was also part of his legacy. The Magnificent Mile became the 5th Avenue of Chicago, an upscale and glittering retail area.

He had a vast portfolio including shopping centers in many cities, as well as office buildings, including 69 W. Washington St. in Chicago. He was a major figure in the development of Carl Sandburg Village, an urban renewal project, consisting of approximately three thousand rental units, seven high-rises, townhouses and low-rises. Sandburg Village bordered on the west end of the Gold Coast and provided a protective shield against problem areas that existed further west.

Mr. Rubloff also founded Arthur Rubloff and Co., a major national real estate company, which he later sold to his employees, although he retained an ownership interest. He told me that in real estate, the money is in development, not in management or brokerage. Charles and Herb Allen were always his partners. Arthur had a private line directly to Charles. I was with him when he would pick up this phone and Charles would be on the other end. He always asked that Herb also be on the line. It is important, he told me, to keep all of the partners fully informed. Arthur explained the details of the deal and the amount of money required. The money became available within 48 hours.

Arthur came to Chicago from Minnesota a poor man. He recognized that real estate was a necessity for businesses, factories and homeowners. He spent an entire life developing his expertise and knowledge to real estate. From an impoverished background, he became an extremely wealthy man. He lived an extravagant life-style, with special condominiums in Chicago, Manhattan and Palm Beach. He had a full-time chauffeur to drive his limousines. He made a point of attending all major social functions and, wearing his derby, became an easily recognizable figure. He was frequently known as one of the ten best-dressed men in the U.S.

In 1979, Arthur sold Sandburg Village to me for $105 million. It was reported to be the highest price ever paid for a residential project.

Arthur was generous to many charitable causes over many decades. He donated his vast collection of valuable paperweights and original sculptures to the Art Institute of Chicago. His will required that his entire estate be distributed within a certain period of time, so that an ongoing bureaucracy would not be established.

Arthur explained that in the real estate business, people gravitate to profes-sionals who exhibit success. His chauffeured car, his manner of dress and wealthy lifestyle were part of his image. He earned it, kept it, and it was profitable.

Besides real estate, Arthur had few other interests. Because of his lifelong dedi-cation to real estate, his mind was active and he was physically capable. He died in 1986 at age 90. I was with Arthur for many years and he never smoked, never drank and never gambled.

LESSONS TO BE LEARNED

1. Lifelong dedication to real estate, for which there is always a great demand, proved very profitable.

2. His financial partners, Charles and Herb Allen, gave Arthur the ability to negotiate deals without having to tell the seller that financing had to be obtained in order to make the purchase. This was a great advantage.

3. The Allens were totally informed of all of Arthur's activities on a current and ongoing basis.

4. He had a great creative mind, as witnessed by many projects throughout the country.

5. He remained young at heart and in mind because his creative mind and physical strength was devoted to real estate, his area of great love. He had no other outside interests.

6. His extravagant lifestyle was an important way of attracting partners and clients in real estate.

CONGRATULATIONS! NOW, WHAT ABOUT YOUR FUTURE?

Congratulations: You have followed my advice, worked hard, and are now a wealthy and successful entrepreneur. You may be wondering: What should I do now?

1. CASH IN YOUR CHIPS?

This will leave you with a great deal of money, but unless you have planned in advance what to do with your leisure time and money, you may not be very happy. A friend of mine built a successful business, cashed in his chips, and later told me that he felt he had made a mistake. What was he going to do with his time?

2. RETIREMENT—WHAT A WONDERFUL OPPORTUNITY

For the first time in many years, you can now pursue various areas of interest. Don't spend all of your leisure time playing golf, tennis or engaging in similar pursuits. Leisure and recreation are important, but your active mind will gradually start to deteriorate. You have proven yourself. I would strongly suggest that you think about the following:

A. Traveling with your spouse.

B. Take classes at the local colleges.

C. Take classes in your religion.

D. Teach. I myself became Professor (adjunct) at UIC, on a pro-bono basis. I refused to be paid. It was giveback time. What was originally meant to be a two or three years commitment became a wonderful ten-year career. The experience kept my mind active, and sharing my lifelong experience as a lawyer and entrepreneur with my students was important and valuable to them and rewarding for me. You don't have to teach at the university level. Consider the high school or college level. Try it. You will find it wonderful.

E. Write a book about your experiences. Writing a book is difficult, but not impossible. I did it—you can, too.

F. Attend lectures.

G. Pursue other activities to keep your mind active. Otherwise, the aches and pains that accompany the aging years will become magnified. Any of the above pursuits will reduce the impact of these new problems. Keeping busy and engaging your mind is wonderful medicine.

H. Join an exercise club. You will be required to attend classes, and exercise is both beneficial to your body and mind. I have disciplined myself to exercise three to four days a week. Many senior men use walkers or wheelchairs. My lifetime habit of exercising has helped me avoid that problem.

I. The Internet offers a wide world of areas of interest. You will be amazed and pleased at what is available for your future.

J. Start a new business, PERHAPS. Do you again need the pressures of the business world? Think about it. Don't do it unless you want to.

K. During a high-holiday service at my synagogue, I heard a statement to the effect that man, even with his dying grasp, reaches for more. I could have continued my successful condominium conversion business and made millions more. However, I stopped. It was time for my wife and me to set aside years of hard work and the pressures that come with business, and to look ahead. We were looking forward to grandchildren and to finding time to enjoy them. Enough time had been spent pursuing the business world and perhaps more time should have been spent raising my own children.

L. Do you enjoy dancing? If so, go to dancing classes. It's a wonderful leisure activity and you will be in the company of other people

M. Spend time with people. Don't become a hermit. Loneliness is destructive.

N. Find hobbies to pursue along with other people with similar interests. You can even make connections with people via the Internet.

3. BE ACQUIRED

You may have many offers and some of the offers will involve paying you in corporate stock. Don't take only stock. The stock may increase or decrease in value. Always be on the safe side. Obtain a sizeable portion of the selling price in <u>cash</u>.

4. SHOULD I STAY WITH THE NEW COMPANY?

You will probably be very unhappy if you do. It's no longer your company, and while your company was your creation, the new company may only use a portion of your old company in their overall plans. Likewise, you may only be consulted on a limited basis. Consider staying on as a consultant with a fixed contract outlining your time and compensation. Do not expect the new company to use your advice, however. By being forewarned in advance about the possible diminished role you will play in the new corporation, you will avoid great disappointment.

5. SHOULD I ACQUIRE ANOTHER COMPANY?

Perhaps—but you should be very cautious because you are entering into an area that may have undisclosed problems. Retain an experienced larger accounting firm to examine a possible candidate for acquisition. I have seen situations that have been successful, but I've also witnessed failures because the necessary investigations were not made.

6. GOING PUBLIC

An investment adviser can assist you. If you have a venture capitalist partner, they may want to go public and this may be a good way to go. Going public means that by now you have formed a large corporation with different types of stock, including non-voting stock. Your financial advisor can assist you in determining the percentage of voting stock you should own to exercise a considerable degree of control. Perhaps five to ten percent of the voting stock will be sufficient. This will enable you to maintain a degree of input and control.

A NEW DIRECTION FOR AMERICAN ENTREPRENEURSHIP

American industry is currently besieged with pressure from all over the world, from rapidly developing countries like China and India becoming aggressively competitive. The United States has lost many industries and hundreds of thousands of jobs. We need a new direction in order to remain competitive.

The United States has always been a world leader in inventions and entrepreneurship. We have the ability to create a large new class of entrepreneurs that can create new industries, and thereby new jobs. What is needed are the following:

1. Introduce high school students to the possibilities of becoming entrepreneurs. They are young and have curious minds, but they don't know where to start. Classes can be easily developed to give them direction.

2. The perennial question for all entrepreneurs, for a high school student or others, is: "I don't have the start-up capital." The necessary start-up capital is often very small and can be obtained from family or friends. However, I strongly urge that this country undertake funding of young high school students who require only a small amount of initial capital, so that they can start their businesses right away.

The 2006 Nobel Peace Prize winner, Muhammad Yunus, author of the auto-biographical *Banker to the Poor*, a small banker in Bangladesh, recognized that women are natural born entrepreneurs. He formed the Grameen Bank, which began providing each woman with a small amount of capital, usually the equivalent of $100. No security or promissory note was required. It started with 42 women in the year 1976 and has extended to approximately 4 million women in 47,836 villages throughout Bangladesh, and has improved the economy tremendously. The payback rate is approximately ninety-eight percent.

Other countries are now following the lead of Muhammad Yunus. Funds are available in this country from many foundations to meet the various requirements of the recipients. Once the proposal has been accepted, no promissory note or collateral is required. The amounts contributed by the foundations vary. It has proven to be a most successful program over many decades. The concept, called microcredit, or microfinancing, has grown internationally.

Why can't the United States follow the lead of these foundations by providing funds in the thousands of high school classes to develop entrepreneurs? The total cost would be extremely small, and the potential benefits to the entrepreneurs and U.S. economy would be great, indeed.

I would strongly urge that you purchase a copy of Yunus' book, *Banker to the Poor*, which is available on Amazon.com for $10.50.

APPENDIX

- Promissory Note Provisions
- Facts For Establishing a Real Estate Office
- Example of Student Business Plan

PROMISSORY NOTE PROVISIONS REQUIRED BY THE LENDER

DEFAULT. I will be in default under this Note if any of the following happen:

Break Other Promises: I break any promise made to Lender or fail to perform promptly at the time and strictly in the manner provided in this Note or in any agreement related to this Note, or in any other agreement or loan I have with Lender.

Default in Favor of Third Parties: I or any Grantor defaults under any loan, extension of credit, security agreement, purchase or sales agreement, or any other agreement, in favor of any other creditor or person that may materially affect any of my property or my ability to repay this Note or perform my obligations under this Note or any of the related documents.

Events Affecting Guarantor: any of the preceding events occurs with respect to any guarantor, endorser, surety, or accommodation party of any of the indebtedness or any guarantor, endorser, surety or accommodation party dies or becomes incompetent, or revokes or disputes the validity of, or liability under, any guaranty of the indebtedness evidenced by this Note.

Insecurity: Lender in good faith believes itself insecure.

LENDERS RIGHTS: Upon default, Lender may declare the entire unpaid principal balance on the Note and all accrued unpaid interest immediately due, and then I will pay that amount.

JURY WAIVER: Lender and I hereby waive the right to any jury trial in any action, proceeding, or counterclaim brought by either Lender or me against the other.

SUCCESSOR AND INTERESTS: the terms of this Note shall be binding upon me, and upon my heirs, personal representatives, successors and assigns, and shall inure to the benefit of the Lender and it's successors and assigns.

FACTS FOR ESTABLISHING A REAL ESTATE OFFICE

Note: Since much of my entrepreneurial career was spent in real estate, I have gathered together some essential notes on the real estate business, which will be helpful should you choose that path yourself.

Class exercise: If you want the same experience my students got in my classes on entrepreneurship, use the facts below to create a business plan for a real estate office. The exercise should give a feel for the sorts of considerations one needs to take into account when starting any sort of business.

Staff
* Secretary
* Salespeople are considered independent contractors. The broker does not have to provide them with insurance or any benefits. They must be provided with a desk and telephones.

Advertising Expense
Advanced by the broker, usually paid for with commissions earned by sales staff.

The selling of real estate in Illinois is paid for by the seller, usually 6%. This however is negotiable in very large transactions. Buyers may also hire the broker and pay the broker a commission.

Other Expenses
Telephones
Rent
Utilities
Liability Insurance

Insurance
It is essential that the broker receive copies of the liability insurance that the sales staff has on their automobiles. In the event of a lawsuit, the broker may be brought in. Also, the broker's liability insurance should have a provision that covers the sales staff.

Other facts
Sales staff should be able to draw against future earnings for a period of approximately six months. Thereafter, the commission earned should be sufficient for the salesperson.

Arrangements should be made to repay the draw advanced from as commissions are earned by the salesperson.

A portion of the 6% commissions may be split with the sales person who obtains the listing. In some offices, sales agents specialize in obtaining listings and their earnings may be substantially more than the sales staff.

The broker should be a member of the Multiple Listing Service. This contains a continuous inventory of properties that are for sale. Included will be information as to recent sales, price reductions and other extremely important information.

Some listing services contain information on properties for sale in various areas of the United States. Real estate is a local business. It is essential that you become knowledgeable or even an expert on the real estate in your locality. I would suggest a radius of no more than 100 miles from your office.

Specialize in one area of real estate. I would suggest residential, which includes townhouses and condominiums. Office buildings and industrial and shopping centers are specialties and require a greater knowledge.

FARMLAND is unproductive unless you can study and understand the growth of large metropolis areas, where the builders will require the purchase of farmland, at a subsequent date. This too is a specialty and requires a great deal of capital and staying power.

Being a salesperson is not a nine-to-five job. Appointments are frequently made in the evening. You are there to service the seller and the buyer.

The buyer or seller may frequently ask you for the name of a real estate lawyer. Refer them to the real estate broker.

There is a great deal of lead-time required from the time the sale is made until the closing. It can take anywhere up to six months. Therefore the salesperson's earnings may be delayed.

These facts are based upon the information given to my class in 1995. It is now 2007. The figures are for 1995 and I want you to use those numbers in doing your business plan. Then you will be able to compare your business plan with the outstanding paper from one of my teams. Obviously, in 2007, all of these numbers would have increased substantially. However, it is not essential for you in preparing a business plan.

Use the numbers I gave my students in 1995.

Capital Required By Broker
$35,000 at 10%
$5,000 contributed by broker

Capital Equipment List		Annual Leasing Expense
1.	6 desks	$1200
2.	6 chairs	$600
3.	1 fax machine	$240
4.	2 computers	$3,000
5.	1 copy machine	$600
6.	Telephone	$360
7.	Office supplies	$100

As a lawyer, I represented real estate brokers for approximately fifteen years. The most successful brokers are those that work long hours and work closely with the sales staff. Most salespeople are not sufficiently knowledgeable about the various methods of financing a purchase. The broker must become an expert and thereby assist his staff.

There is an old saying—IF THE BUYER CANNOT PAY FOR IT, NO MATTER HOW GREAT THE VALUE, IT WILL NOT BE SOLD.

Desks, computers can be leased or purchased by the broker. I would suggest where a broker has limited capital to lease the computers, copying equipment, etc., because the equipment frequently becomes outdated in approximately two to three years. Preserve your capital. Leasing is an inexpensive way to go.

There is gold beneath your feet. A knowledgeable broker or salesperson, with proper diligence, can quickly discover a value that they would like to purchase.

The seller must be notified in writing that the salesperson/broker is buying the property. Otherwise, there is a breach of fiduciary relationship.

By studying the listing sheets and watching for properties that have been on the market for a great amount of time, you may be able to determine that a new, reduced selling price makes an excellent value.

In major transactions involving usually office buildings, sales are made on a private basis. A broker will be selected by the sales organization to find a buyer.

Every listing sheet will carry a notice that the information contained was obtained from the seller and is not guaranteed to be accurate by the broker/salesperson.

Structure
Corporation
Broker to own 100% of stock

Professionals
Accountant & lawyer (Use small firms)

I strongly suggest that the broker require each member of the sales staff to join various local organizations such as church groups, fraternal institutions and so on so that this person becomes known in the community for being real estate salespeople.

<u>Income</u>
The office secretary will assist the salesperson with their appointments, updating appointments and other details.

<u>Location</u>
The real estate office should be on a major street easily identifiable by both buyer and seller. The office should be on the ground floor with parking nearby.

<u>Other expenses</u>
Advertising by broker—$500 or more per month, depending upon activity
Insurance (office, liability, equipment) $300 per month
Furniture and equipment rental—$200 to $400 per month
Usual office rent—$1200 per month
Grand-opening (one-time cost) $2,000

A grand opening gives the broker and staff the opportunity to obtain coverage in local newspapers and media. The broker should invite the local clergymen, media reporters. It should be a gala event with food and soft beverages (NO liquor).

Printing stationery (one-time cost) $1,000
Office supplies—$75 per month
Telephones—$500 per month
Utilities—$250 per month
Entertainment—$200 per month

SAMPLE BUSINESS PLAN

Names and addresses have been removed to protect the privacy of the students who created this business plan.

INITIAL REALTY
123 Highway
Chicago, Illinois 00000
(123) 456-7890

Team III

STATEMENT OF PURPOSE

To establish Initial Realty, a real estate brokerage, as the top seller of real estate, in the high demand North Shore area. Initial Realty will primarily sell residential property.

TABLE OF CONTENTS

I.   THE BUSINESS

    A.   Description of Business

    B.   Product/Service

    C.   Market

    D.   Location of Business

    E.   Competition

    F.   Management

    G.   Personnel

    H.   Application and Expected Effect of Loan

    I.   Summary

II.   FINANCIAL DATA

    A.   Sources and Applications of Funding

    B.   Capital Equipment List

    C.   Balance Sheet

    D.   Break-Even Analysis

    E.   Income Projections (Profit and Loss Statements)

        1.   Number of Homes Sold

        2.   Quarterly Income Projection—Year 2

        3.   Quarterly Income Projection—Year 3

THE BUSINESS

<u>Description of Business</u>

Initial Realty is a real estate brokerage firm selling primarily residential homes. Initial Realty is a business of five people:

1. The broker, or head of the business
2. Manager in charge of the daily operations of the office
3. Three salespeople

The broker provides the essential resources to the agents, who in turn, split the commissions on the sales with the broker.

<u>Product/Service</u>

Initial Realty provides many services to the sellers and buyers and residential property. These services include:

1. Look for sellers
2. Attempt to find buyers
3. Advertise (MLS, newspaper, signs)
4. Provide open houses
5. Assist in document preparation
6. Provide accurate market evaluation
7. Work with both sides to agree to a sale
8. Assist in closing of the sale

<u>Market</u>

Our market niche consists of residential property. We will list property throughout the Chicagoland area, however, we will specialize in the North Shore area of suburban Chicago. The North Shore area is an area of high demand. In the last decade, some areas have more than doubled in appreciation; we contribute this to the low crime rate (in eight towns alone there were less than 5 violent crimes). The North Shore area also has nationally ranked schools. (New Trier, Deerfield, Highland Park and Lake Forest). The North Shore area also has strong police protection, which is evidenced by their low crime rate.

Location of Business

Initial Realty is located at 123 Highway Road. It is a highly visible office on the main street in Glenview. It is one of six business storefronts. There is ample parking for all employees and up to 15 customers at any one time. Initial Realty is located next to two main grocery stores and McDonald's.

Competition

The main competitors of Initial Realty will be Century 21, Koenig & Strey, and Kahn Realty. The realtors are the main realtors of the North Shore area. By the end of our first year in business, we intend to only be in competition with Century 21.

Management

John Doe, a licensed realtor, will be in charge of the management of our business. He will also sell homes, and will receive full commission for his sales, thus forgoing an annual salary. He has ten years of sales experience, including five years on the North Shore.

Personnel

Referring back to the description of our business, we are a group of five people:

1. _____, Licensed broker and head of organization
2. _____, Manager and also a licensed broker
3. _____, Salesperson
4. _____, Salesperson
5. _____, Salesperson
6. Three secretaries

Initial Realty is a company with 45 years of real estate experience, including 25 years of North Shore sales experience.

Application and Expected Effect of Loan

Initial Realty is seeking a loan to start our business for the purpose of covering our initial start-up costs and expenses incurred during the first 2-3 quarters of our first fiscal year (April 30). We will need a $35,000 loan at 10% interest over 5 years. This loan should cover our costs until the closing of our homes sales, which will be approximately 4-6 months after business resumes.

<u>Summary</u>

The average home value in Glenview is $257,000 and the average home value in neighboring towns is $200,000–$600,000. There were 5 violent crimes and 891 thefts last year, which is relatively low. The average income of Glenview is $75,000. We feel that income streams will remain high in the North Shore community. Growing appreciation because of it's relative location to Chicago, as well as low crime, good schools, and attractive surroundings will keep this trend dissipating in the long term.

FINANCIAL DATA

Sources and Application of Funding

Initial Realty will borrow $35,000 at 10%. The broker will contribute $5,000 to the business. The cash investment and loan proceeds will cover start up costs; applied, but not limited to, advertising, rental of the office equipment, rental of office space and supplies.

Capital Equipment List	Annual Leasing Expense
1. 6 desks	$1,200
2. 6 chairs	$600
3. 1 fax machine	$240
4. 2 computers	$3,000
5. 1 copy machine	$600
6. Telephone	$360

BALANCE SHEET

MAY 1, 1995

ASSETS

Current Assets:

Cash	$39,900
Commission receivable	$ 0
Office Supplies	$ 100
Total Current Assets	$40,000

Fixed Assets:

	- 0 -
TOTAL ASSETS	$40,000

LIABILITIES

Current liabilities:

Current due loan payment	- 0 -
Total current liabilities	- 0 -
Long-Term Liabilities	$35,000
TOTAL LIABILITES	**$35,000**

EQUITY

Contributed Capital	$5,000
TOTAL LIABILITES AND EQUITY	$40,000

BREAK EVEN ANALYSIS

	MONTH 1	MONTH 2	MONTH 3	MONTH 4	MONTH 5	MONTH 6
REVENUE	*-0-*	*-0-*	*-0-*	*-0-*	*$13,500*	*$18000*
EXPENSES	$8,820	$8,820	$8,820	$8,820	$14,220	$16,020
	LOSS	LOSS	LOSS	LOSS	LOSS	BREAK-EVEN

INCOME PROJECTIONS

	May	June	July	August	September	October	November	December	January	February	March	April
Revenue	0	0	0	0	13,500	18,000	18,000	18,000	18,000	18,000	18,000	13,000
Expenses:												
Agent's Commission	0	0	0	0	5,400	7,200	7,200	7,200	7,200	7,200	7,200	5,400
Broker's Salary	2,000	2,000	2,000	2,000	2,000	2,000	2,000	2,000	2,000	2,000	2,000	2,000
Other Salary	1,852	1,852	1,852	1,852	1,852	1,852	1,852	1,852	1,852	1,852	1,852	1,852
Loan	748	748	748	748	748	748	748	748	748	748	748	748
Rent	1,000	1,000	1,000	1,000	1,000	1,000	1,000	1,000	1,000	1,000	1,000	1,000
Utilities	300	300	300	300	300	300	300	300	300	300	300	300
Phone	300	300	300	300	300	300	300	300	300	300	300	300
Advertising	500	500	500	500	500	500	500	500	500	500	500	500
Leased Equipment	500	500	500	500	500	500	500	500	500	500	500	500
Office Supplies	100	100	100	100	100	100	100	100	100	100	100	100
Entertainment	50	50	50	50	50	50	50	50	50	50	50	50
Misc.	1,470	1,470	1,470	1,470	1,470	1,470	1,470	1,470	1,470	1,470	1,470	1,470
Total Expenses	8,820	8,820	8,820	8,820	14,220	16,020	16,020	16,020	1,620	16,020	16,020	14,220
Profit/Loss	(8,820)	(8,820)	(8,820)	(8,820)	(720)	1,980	1,980	1,980	1,980	1,980	1,980	(720)

NUMBER OF HOMES SOLD

	MAY	JUNE	JULY	AUG.	SEPT.	OCT.	NOV.	DEC.	JAN.	FEB.	MARCH
# OF HOMES	0	0	0	0	3	4	4	4	4	4	3

AVERAGE SELLING PRICE OF EACH HOME—$150,000
COMMISSIONS ARE BASED ON 6% OR $9,000, WITH 3% OR $4,500 GOING TO THE BROKER THAT LISTED THE HOUSE
DURING OUR FIRST YEAR OF OPERATION WE DO NOT EXPECT TO LIST ANY HOUSES. DURING OUR SECOND YEAR OF OPERATION, WE EXPECT TO LIST 25% OF THE HOUSES THAT WE SELL, AND DURING OUR THIRD YEAR OF OPERATION WE EXPECT TO LIST 50% OF THE HOUSES THAT WE SELL.

INCOME PROJECTION—YEAR 2

	1ST Quarter	2nd Quarter	3rd Quarter	4th Quarter
REVENUE	$67,500	$67,500	$67,500	$67,500
EXPENSE	$53,460	$53,460	$53,460	$53,460
PROFIT	$14,040	$14,040	$14,040	$14,040

INCOME PROJECTION—YEAR 3

	1ST Quarter	2nd Quarter	3rd Quarter	4th Quarter
REVENUE	$112,500	$112,500	$112,500	$112,500
EXPENSE	$71,460	$71,460	$71,460	$71,460
PROFIT	$41,040	$41,040	$41,040	$41,040

NOTES OF EXPLANATION: The first year Initial Realty sold 30 homes @$150,00 (average price), none of which were our listings. The second year we sold 36 homes with the average value of $200,000, which were 25% our listings, 75% other listings. The third year we sold 40 homes at the average value of $250,000 with 50% of our listings and 50% other listings.

MANDATORY READING

The Business Planning Guide
David H. Bangs, Jr.
Dearborn Trade Publishing, Chicago
    Mr. Bangs, a highly successful entrepreneur, has written a guideline, which is simple and helpful. Use it.

The World Is Flat: A Brief History of the Twenty-First Century
Thomas L. Friedman, Farrar, Straus and Giroux, 2005.
Obtain newest edition
    Thomas Friedman is a featured writer of the *New York Times*. He is a highly respected journalist. This book has become a best seller because hundreds of thousands are wondering what is happening to the United States in the twenty-first century. Mr. Friedman has his overview of the future. My world, born in 1921, is gone except for memories. The world of my children, all in their fifties, is fixed by their professions and education. Their children, my grandchildren, are facing a new, strange and possibly fearful future. Read this book. Study it. It will help you become prepared.

SUGGESTED READING

You Can Negotiate Anything
Herb Cohen, Lyle Stuart Inc. edition published 1980
    Throughout your life, you will be negotiating. To be successful, you must be negotiating with a sense of power. This book will give you some understanding on why you have power. I have studied this book in my class and also with my eldest grandson. The book has become a best seller, obtainable in soft-cover.

The Great Crash
Professor John Kenneth Galbrath, Houghton Mifflin Company
    A Harvard professor now in his nineties and still active, *The Great Crash* was a monumental study of the Great Crash of 1929 that preceded the Great Depression. Our system of capitalism has periods of recessions and occasionally, a serious recession, called a depression. By his careful analysis of the ingredients of the Great Crash, you will be able to recognize some of the symptoms and warnings of forthcoming recessions and you should be able to protect yourself. I used this book to avoid problems because I could recognize the dangers of upcoming recessions.

Some of the Wall Street firms are still in existence. It is a short book and can possibly save your life's fortune. I read this book many years ago and gained insights which protected me and my capital from the recurring problem of recessions in our economic system. Obtain a copy, possibly through Harvard University as a resource. Read it, study it. It may be one of the most important books you will ever read.

Manias, Panics and Crashes: A History of Financial Crises
Charles P. Kindleberger, John Wiley & Sons, Inc.
This author, a highly respected economist, reviews economic recessions beginning prior to the Great Crash of 1929. This will give you a greater understanding of the reoccurrence of recessions in our capitalistic society.

The Entrepreneurial Imperative
Carl J. Schram, President, The Kauffman Foundation
Harper Collins, 2006

How About A Career In Real Estate?
Carla Cross, Dearborn Financial Publishing, 1993
This publisher also has many other business publications; obtain their catalog.

Real Estate Investing from A to Z
William H. Pivar, McGraw-Hill

Real Estate Newsletter
Robert J. Bruss, JD
Attorney at Law
251 Park Road, Suite 200
Burlingame, CA 94919-4228
I have been subscribing to this newsletter for over twenty-five years. Each newsletter either refreshes my recollection or gives me new ideas that are important. A catalog of his newsletters is available. I would strongly suggest that you obtain the entire list, because you will be going back and finding other items that are important if you are going to be involved in the real estate field.

RESOURCES FOR THE RESOURCEFUL ENTREPRENEUR

BOOKS

What No One Ever Tells You About Starting Your Own Business:
Real Life Start-Up Advice from 101 Successful Entrepreneurs
Jan Norman, Dearborn Trade (November 1998)

Start Your Own Business
(Entrepreneur Magazine's Start Up) (Paperback)
Rieva Lesonsky, Entrepreneur Press; 3rd edition (March 24, 2004)

The Entrepreneurial Mindset
Rita Gunther McGrath, Ian MacMillan
Harvard Business School Press (August 2000)

Harvard Business Review on Entrepreneurship
(Harvard Business Review Paperback Series) (Paperback)
Amar Bhldt, William Sahlman, James Stancil, Arthur Rock, Michael Nevens,
Gregory Summe
Harvard Business School Press (February 1999)

The Street Smart Entrepreneur: 133 Tough Lessons I Learned the Hard Way
(Paperback)
Jay Goltz, Addicus Books (1998)

Innovation and Entrepreneurship
Peter F. Drucker
Collins; 1st edition (May 26, 1993)

PUBLICATIONS

Entrepreneur magazine
http://www.entrepreneur.com/magazine/entrepreneur/index.html

BizJournal: Entrepreneurship
http://www.bizjournals.com/entrepreneur/

Minority Business Entrepreneur magazine
http://www.mbemag.com/

Be Successful News
http://www.ksinclair.com/pbs_news.htm

Entrepreneur Digest
http://www.talkbiz.com/digest/

OTHER WEB SOURCES

Wikipedia
http://en.wikipedia.org/wiki/Entrepreneur

Entrepreneur Help Page
http://www.tannedfeet.com/

Vocational Information Center
http://www.khake.com/page31.html

Entrepreneurship for young people
http://www.youngentrepreneur.com/

The Entrepreneur's Mind
http://www.benlore.com/

Entrepreneur's Organization (EO)
http://www.eonetwork.org/

Entrepreneur America
http://www.entrepreneur-america.com/

978-0-595-43742-9
0-595-43742-7